# Bottles to Backpacks: The Gypsy Mama's Guide to *Real* Travel With Kids

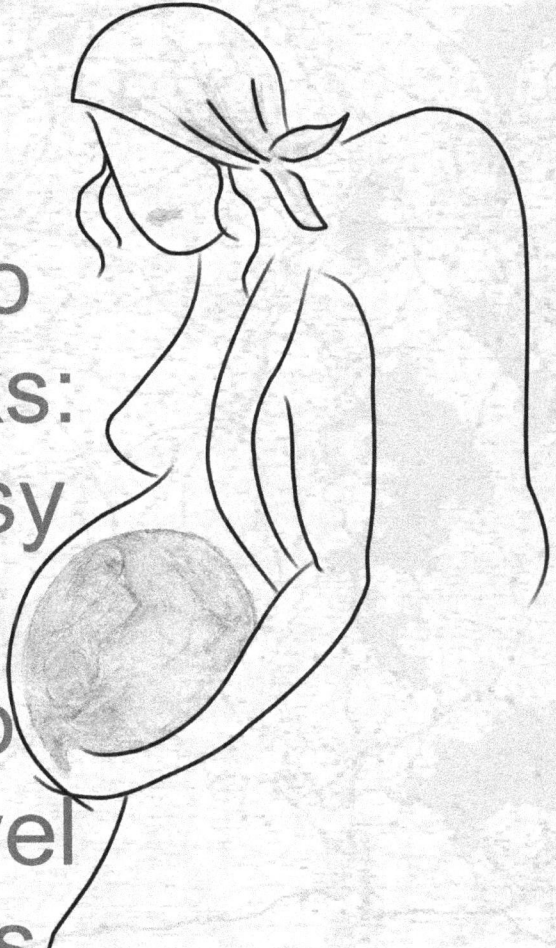

by Jenn Miller &
Keri Wellman

# Bottles to Backpacks:

## The Gypsy Mama's Guide to Real Travel With Kids

by: Jennifer Miller and Keri Wellman

ISBN: 978-0-9852771-3-0

# TABLE OF CONTENTS

## Chapter 4: Accommodation Options

## Chapter 5: Preparing to Travel

# Travel with Babies

## Chapter 6: Intro to Baby Travel

## Chapter 7: It All Starts At Home!

## Chapter 8: Packing & Carriers

## Chapter 9: Help! I've Got A Screamer!

# Travel with Toddlers

## Chapter 10: Intro to Toddler Travel

## Chapter 11: Travel Train Your Toddler

## Chapter 12: Managing Behavior

## Chapter 13: Picky Eaters & Travel

## Chapter 14: Potty Training & Travel

## Chapter 15: Outsmarting Your Toddler 101

# Travel with School-Agers

## Chapter 16: Intro to School Age Travel

## Chapter 17: Safety Plans

## Chapter 18: Preparing To Travel

## Chapter 19: Life On The Road

## Chapter 20: Educational Opportunities

## Chapter 21: Out Of The Mouths Of Babes

# Travel with Teens

## Chapter 22: Travel With All Sorts of Teens

## Chapter 23: Getting Your Teen On Board

## Chapter 24: Travel As Education

## Chapter 25: A Question of Freedom

## THE WAY WE TRAVEL: Hints Tips & Gear

## ADDITIONAL RESOURCES & LINKS

# INTRODUCTION

Big-time World Travel: it's always been your dream. You imagine yourself taking early morning walks on the beach before settling under your favorite palm tree to work for a few hours; touring art museums; or climbing ancient ruins by day and working your business in the evening hours, which are your most productive anyway. You dreamt of apartment-hopping across Europe and Asia; or working from your boat, moored in Vanuatu, and sending exotic postcards to your friends back home—dreams that came to a screeching halt with the arrival of two pink lines and the impending arrival of... your baby.

You rally briefly and think to yourself, "I can manage this; it's only a baby. It won't be that bad. I can still travel. I can still live my dreams."

Then you tell your friends, some of whom already have children, and you are met with incredulous stares:

"Of COURSE you can't take a baby traveling! This is going to change your life FOREVER. Enjoy your freedom while you have it! Life as you know it is about to END. You have NO IDEA what you're getting into!"

*"Buy a house. Settle down. Baton down the hatches. Dig in. Spend a thousand dollars on brightly colored plastic 'must haves.' It's all over but the cryin'!"*

*They can't all be wrong... can they?*

1

We're here to tell you they are wrong. We're living proof they're wrong, and we'll show you how you transform your baby-bump-in-the road into a baby-bump ON the road.

Of course adding a child to the mix of a nomadic life adds an element of challenge that didn't exist before. Children have very real needs that must be respected, met and managed; and it's our responsibility as parents to put those first in our minds.

Life does change with children--for the better. It's true we have no idea what we're getting into when we have our first babies, but we learn and grow together. Kids do require infrastructure and gear, but not as much as you think.

Be encouraged, and read on! We'll walk you through the basics, from packing to health care, and before you know it, you'll be proving those naysayers wrong--just like we are.

# MEET THE GYPSY MAMAS

First, we'd like to introduce ourselves, so you'll know who we are and believe us when we say, "We've been there, done that!"

Zaafrane, Tunisia, Winter 2008

## Jenn Miller

I was raised by nomadic parents in the back of a van across North America. I took my first solo trip, three weeks in the UK, when I was just sixteen. I married my knight in shining armor at the tender age of nineteen and together we've lead a life of epic adventure that is so much better than I could ever have dreamt.

We have four kids, currently aged 8-14, our oldest, Hannah, is a girl, the younger ones are boys.

**The "stats" on our youngest:**

- First international border crossing: 3 weeks old
- First cross continental flight: 5 weeks old
- By 6 months his feet had been dipped in the Atlantic, Pacific and the Hawaiian shores of the Pacific; and he'd logged enough air miles to qualify for priority seating!
- At 3 he made a 500 mile cycle trip, and even helped pedal for most of it!
- At 5 we made him homeless and embarked on a year-long cycle tour of Europe and North Africa (the other kids went too).
- He can tell me "no" in seven languages.

I've walked, cycled, flown, road-tripped, and ridden train with babies through teens. I've dealt with temper tantrums in every single country. For the past three years we've lived on the road full time, which means that traveling with kids, literally, is my life.

**Trust me when I say, "You can do this!"**

## Keri Wellman

I was a typical Midwestern girl until the travel bug bit. When I graduated high school, I swapped my car for tickets to Europe. It was the trip of a lifetime: Germany, Switzerland, Italy. When I boarded the airplane to go back to America, I knew in my broken teenage heart, I would never see Europe again.

A few years later love swept me to Alaska, where I had four children in scarcely six years.

Once or twice a year. I could be found schlepping through Anchorage International Airport with: slings, strollers, or backpacks; pregnant; alone; with my husband; with one baby; with one baby and a toddler; with two preschoolers and a baby; or with one kindergartner, a preschooler, a toddler, and a baby.

After 12 years in Alaska, a major lifestyle change allowed us to roadschool from Alaska, to Iowa, to Arizona, to the Florida Panhandle. Our kids were 8, 7, 3, and 2 years-old when we brushed the white sand from our feet and boarded a plane to Germany.

Now, with a quiet Franconian village as our base, we take advantage of the ease-of-travel in Europe.

**By the ripe-old age of six, my youngest has:**

Been taken up the 287 steps of St. Vitt cathedral in a backpack

- Smelled the spring flowers of Keukenhoff Gardens
- Been mesmerized by West End theater
- Climbed the Eifel Tower
- Studied original DaVincis, Botticellis and Michelangelos
- Explored catacombs, necropoli and amphitheaters
- counted horses on Etruscan funeraries
- Trekked through catacombs
- Climbed on ancient ruins; counted horses on Etruscan funeraries
- Swam in turquoise alpine lakes
- Fallen asleep on the floor of a Venetian gondola
- Sung along with Papageno in Mozart's hometown
- More importantly however, her travels have opened her eyes to the preciousness of people from many different cultures.

**Traveling with children is difficult work. But it is worth the effort when I witness my two sons and two daughters thinking as young citizens of the world.**

# WHY TRAVEL WITH KIDS?

Before we get into the nitty gritty of how to make it happen and how to juggle all of the aspects of travel with a kids of various ages, let's talk for just a minute about WHY people in their right minds would WANT to travel with a tiny person, beyond a two-week vacation.

There are lots of reasons why, actually, not the least of which is: it was your dream!

Here are a few benefits to traveling with children to mull over as we move along:

- Travel teaches flexibility (even for babies)
- The sights, sounds and colors of international places will help form your child's emerging concept of the world
- Natural introduction of the sounds of multiple languages can impact language development
- A range of foods and tastes helps broaden your toddler's palate (and minimize picky eating)
- Builds a feeling of world citizenship: your child will learn to feel comfortable cross-culturally
- Children build bridges with the locals--they're often your ticket into a community

Besides all that, traveling with kids means you'll get priority seating, and that's why you became a parent, right, for what the kid could do for you?

Traveling with kids is NOT easy. Anyone who says it is, either has only done it once when the travel stars were properly aligned, or he's lying.

**There are, however, very real benefits, for you and for your child.**

Looking at the world through the eyes of your baby as she grows, learns and explores will open your eyes and heart anew to the wonderful blend of nature and culture that surrounds us everywhere we go.

Let's face it, as adults, we get jaded.

Traveling with our kids forces us to slow down, notice the little things, and appreciate the amazing differences and wonderful diversity that is The World.

Don't miss all of that by staying home!

# THE BASICS

## Get Your Ducks In A Row

My Uncle Dick has a saying that applies to just about every aspect of world travel, even more so if you have kids: "Remember the 7 P's."

"What are the 7 P's?" you ask: **Proper Prior Planning Prevents Piss Poor Performance.**

Write it down. Tattoo it on your lower back. Embroider it on the diaper bag. Remember it: those are your words to live by.

Spontaneity is not out of the question when traveling with kids, but it isn't going to flow smoothly until you've mastered the art of planning for every single possible contingency. Plan now. Be spontaneous later.

## What Should I Plan For?

Great question! So many parents choose not to travel with their kids because they are overwhelmed by the mountain of details that surrounds even a weekend away with small children.

The good news is that it's not as bad as it seems at first glance.

The remainder of this book will guide you through:

- Packing & gear
- Healthcare before you leave and abroad
- Transportation
- Lodging
- Maintaining comfort and routines
- Education
- Entertainment
- Staying connected
- Preparing your child for the realities and discomforts of travel
- Dietary concerns
- And much more...

We'll hold your hand and walk you through your first trip abroad with your tiny baby, and we'll give you ideas for how to create the educational adventure of a lifetime with your teenagers.

No matter what ages your children are, NOW is the perfect time to pack your bags and venture out into the great big world. They grow up too fast and now is the only moment we have... don't miss it!

# CHAPTER 1: GEAR & PACKING

## Three Words: Less Is More.

We've all seen THAT family at the airport: Dad with baby in backpack and computer bag is wrestling eight large bags off the luggage carousel, while Mom balances a car seat on top a stroller loaded with a nappie sack stuffed to the max, whilst holding the hand of a toddler who's bouncing at the end of her arm like a ping pong ball. They nervously count bags and try to shove the contents of the bag with the split zipper into the outer pouches of the other bags. How two adults and two little kids will manage to haul eight overloaded bags and a backpack each to the shuttle (much less their final destination) is a mystery to all.

It is precisely that image which causes most new parents with wanderlust to hyperventilate with the mere thought of: "I've been reduced to THIS?!" No wonder traveling with kids has a bad rap.

Right next to that family is a sleek Gypsy Mama with twin eight year olds, carrying their own backpacks, and a 9 month old baby tied securely on her hip, gumming a chew toy. She's got a shoulder bag the size of a normal purse. She lifts one medium sized bag off of the carousel and rolls it gently toward the bus stop. No baby gear in sight.

Which one would you rather be?

11

**It's easy to understand how the first poor family ended up needing a camel to get through the airport, never mind the joy of using public transportation with that amount of gear. A quick internet search on traveling with kids will yield "pack lists" that are downright demoralizing.**

I'm going to let you in on the secrets of the second Mama:

**She rents it all.**

- If you're flying into anywhere and going to be renting a car, you can get it with the appropriate sized car seat strapped right into the backseat for you.
- If you're staying in a hotel, or even many hostels, you simply pre-book a pack-n-play style crib when you make your reservation.
- If you're staying longer, say six months, make your first stop a children's resale shop and buy only the most necessary items.
- Donate them to the needy when you fly back out.

If you too are a Gypsy Mama and plan to travel for a lifestyle, then a few, well chosen, pieces of kid travel gear make an excellent investment that pays off in ease and peace for everyone. What are these?

# For Babies & Toddlers

**A sling:** A simple, old-school sling. I know there a million "Mama torture devices" as my friend calls the myriad of baby carriers on the market. I tried a bunch of them. I hated them all.

For ease of use, multi-functionality, and value, the basic sling is still the best kid-carrier on the market. I've toted kids, newborn through five years old comfortably on my back across continents in mine.

It doubles as a play blanket, a changing pad, a nursing cover up, a burp cloth, and a diaper bag if you buy the one made by a <u>mother of seven in New Hampshire</u>… she sews pockets in the ends so there's enough room for a couple of diapers, wipes, a bottle and a small toy. She's a genius. Buy two so you're never without.

A pack-n-play, playpen: I know, I just told you to rent it, or buy it on site, and that's still the best plan. BUT, if you have a child who is very sensitive to changes in location and is one of those poor elves that cries all night in unfamiliar territory, one antidote is to make every new destination feel like home. This is easily accomplished by taking your own playpen and sheets (that smell familiar) to make your little one comfortable.

Ease of travel is important, but needs of the baby are paramount. If one extra checked bag means peace and happiness, then it's a small price to pay. This was very important to one of our babies, so we bought the most portable crib we could find; and it was money well spent.

## For Older Kids

**A Backpack:** One solid backpack each, for carrying their personal items. Don't get the cheap, ten dollar kind, get a solid, thirty dollar LLBean, Land's End or JanSport variety with a leather or heavy canvas bottom, YYK zippers and proper straps. They'll last for years, and you'll thank yourself.

## The One Bag Rule

The sleek Gypsy Mama has one more secret to her smooth travel routine: **She's an adherent to the "One Bag Rule."**

What is the one bag rule? Exactly what it sounds like. **You get ONE bag for the whole family. Period.**

The fine print:

- If there are six or fewer in your family you get ONE bag. It can be the biggest bag you can find, but ONE only. If you have seven people or more, you can have an extra bag.
- If you are going for three weeks or less: ONE bag. A trip of one month or longer: two bags.
- If you are going to travel through more than one climate zone, this also earns an extra bag.
- If you are participating in gear heavy sports (like SCUBA) you may take an extra bag for that gear.

**What you do NOT get an extra bag for: having a baby.**

Maybe you're shaking your head now, thinking, "What is she NUTS?! That's impossible!" I point you back to the two families: which do you want to be?

Long term and lifestyle travel is simply not sustainable if you are bogged down with ten bags for a family of four (and most families are!) Dealing with lost baggage, too much baggage, heavy baggage on public transport, packing and unpacking are the biggest joy stealers and time wasters of traveling. **Less is more.**

One bag for a family of six or fewer is NOT impossible--it's totally doable, and it simplifies EVERYTHING.

**What goes in the bag:**

Three changes of clothes per person (five for a baby)

- Toiletries
- Swim suits
- Two comfort items for your child; blankie and bear, perhaps?
- Secondary sling (if you have a child under 5 years-old)
- Mini-package of wipes for emergencies

- A two pack of extra soothers (pacifiers) if you have a baby
- First aid kit
- Educational Supplies
- Rubber ball (universal sink stopper for hand washing clothes in the hotel tub.)
- That's it.

"Ahh, but there is so much my baby and I NEED that you've left out!" I hear you replying. Yes, there is, and ALL of it can be had virtually anywhere in the world.

Diapers, food, creams, soaps, brushes, rash ointments, extra bottles, sippy cups, wipes, crayons and pencils and the million other prepackaged niceties we've all come to believe we MUST HAVE are available in one form or another anywhere there are children. if you're willing to be flexible about brands. Don't pack ANY of that stuff. Buy it when you get there.

If there is ONE thing you can do to make travel with baby more fun and less stressful it is this: **Pack less. One bag. It's all you need. We promise.**

## Alternatives To the One Bag Rule

There are times when packing one bag for the entire family is not the most convenient option.

If you're taking a short trip, of a week or less, you might want each child to carry his own clothing and toiletries in his regular sized backpack.

Or, if you're taking off for six months of backpacking in Central America, like we did, you might want each family member to have his own "real" backpack for the adventure.

The advantages of each child having his own bag are many:

It teaches personal responsibility

- He learns how to pack appropriately
- She learns to carry her own weight
- It allows your child to learn, by trial and error, what they really need to travel.

### Packing for a road trip

When we go on a road trip that is less than 500 miles, and if space isn't an issue, I do not double-check my older children's bags (aged 9 and up). By this age, they are completely capable of packing themselves without my oversight.

When a child forgets to bring something important, he has to deal with the consequences, such as being uncomfortable, doing extra wash or paying for a replacement with his own funds. If he has to pay for something with his own money (or has to borrow an object from his little brother) he will never leave important items behind again, especially if it is something he doesn't want to share, like a toothbrush!

### The Over Packer

On the other hand, giving your child autonomy in the packing process exposes you to the danger of the over-packer. If you notice your young child's backpack looks as if it has swallowed a baby elephant, by all means, check it out. However, if your child is nine or older and you are going on a short journey, let him over-pack—just once. **The only rule is that under no circumstances do you help him carry the over-packed bag!**

## Keri Says:

One of my children once had a backpack that was nearly bursting at the seams. Though I was curious about all the strange angles poking out, I kept quiet.

My son had to heft the pack from our secured parking garage, across the city, along the steep road next to the park and finally up the three flights of stairs of our apartment in Prague.

While we all laughed when he pulled out the enormous dragon pillow and metal container of ceramic dominoes, he never over-packed again. It was simply too much—and the natural consequences were enough to teach him, without a single negative word from mom.

# Hints For Family Packing

**Color Coordination:** As a family, we agree on a color-scheme (even if the clothes aren't identical), and the children have the option to pack what they like, within the color range.

Color-coordinating began when my kids were small, and I simply thought it was cute to have matching outfits. But I soon realized that not only could I quickly identify my kids in a crowd, but we also looked great together in pictures.

One surprising benefit of traveling with color-coordinated kids is if you have a large family, you are sometimes mistaken for a school group and security guards will lead you to a significantly shorter line (seriously, this has happened to us more than once in both Paris and Rome).

**Have A Pack List:** Even if the pack-list is short, make one for your kids so they can check it off as they go. It is something concrete they can do to be part of the traveling process.

If your child cannot yet read, draw pictures on the pack list. I am always amused to watch my little ones unpack their bags when we arrive somewhere because they know exactly what is in the bag, and they control where items should go—it gives them a real sense of pride (even if their clothes are exactly the same as their older sibling's).

If you have a serious objection to plain white t-shirts and tattered jeans, make sure you tell your child before he packs. You may think it illogical to pack pants where the patches in the knees are worn clean through, but your twelve year-old son might think otherwise.

## Jenn Says:

We began color coordinating our kids when we had four under four.

We found that we were treated differently when they were dressed alike: "Oh, are they all yours? They're so CUTE! They look like the VonTrapps! Do they sing!!" instead of "OH... those are ALL yours... ugh...better YOU than me." Yes, people really are that rude.

In addition to ensuring a smoother reception of our growing tribe, like Keri, we discovered it made our kids easy to spot in a crowd.

We once lost Elisha (then five) in a two block square, two story mercado in Merida, Mexico. It was a LONG twenty minutes while we searched for him. Ultimately, his matching clothes were what helped strangers find him!

# Packing Carry-On Bags & Personal Items

If your young travelers are high energy, you may question your decision to embark on the travel lifestyle, which often involves being trapped in some form of transit for hours with no escape.

Besides the fear of dealing with behavioral issues, the fear of keeping a child entertained causes many parents to avoid travel until their children graduate and move out. What a shame!

**There are two key ideas regarding packing which will help you in your travels:**

- By the time they are school age, children have the mental capability to entertain themselves with very little outside stimulus.
- Allowing your child to pack her own carry-on bag (even if she has very few choices about what actually goes into it) will help her to feel satisfied with her entertainment options.

These two points are crucial to keep in mind when you travel.

A child should be trained and encouraged to entertain himself through imagination, rather than through an outside source such as Mum, Dad or Nintendo. The child who gets "bored" is the one who has run out of outside stimulus— and trust me, it is impossible to pack for this kid because eventually, he will be bored with it all.

**So what do you do if you have not yet trained your child to do without?**

Take a short trip and leave all the gadgets and gizmos behind.

You don't have to go cold turkey unless your schedule demands it. But practice turning off the television and video games and slowly increase your child's gadget-free time.

There may be fights and tears, but if you remain consistent and don't give in, you'll make it through the withdrawals, and your child will become a much more contented traveler; which means traveling will be more enjoyable for everyone. If they can live without at home, they can live without anywhere!

# What To Pack In A Carry-On

When we go on short trips our children carry their own carry-on sized backpacks. The backpack contains two sets of clothes, one pair of pajamas, socks, underwear, and a toothbrush. Once the basics are packed (and double-checked by mom), the kids are then allowed to bring items for entertainment.

**Objects for entertainment can include...**

- Books or ebook reader
- New colored pencils
- Activity books, such as sudoku, crosswords or our favorite, the "Anti-Coloring Book"
- Sketch pad
- Journal
- Camera
- Playing Cards
- Tape
- Travel-sized chess set
- Toys small enough to fit into a zip-top bag
- iPod or iTouch for music, audio books & communication (with limited use)

## The Secret Weapon:

What is it? It is a secret stash of things sure to entertain, amuse, intrigue, distract, wow, or otherwise keep a kid busy  when you REALLY need it. The greatest power of this weapon lies in its secrecy. If the child KNOWS the weapon exists, it will be far less amazing to its intended target, and all benefits of the weapon will be outweighed by the major detractor of the child ASKING for it every five seconds. What should you load it with:

- balloons
- tiny toys
- rubber bouncy balls
- a deck of cards
- fun pad activity books
- a new story to read aloud
- a few postcards to write home to friends
- stickers & paper
- a magnetic travel game or puzzle
- bubbles (not for in the car or airplane!)
- scotch tape, hours of fun!
- old hotel key cards (kids love these!)

To deploy the weapon, bring out just ONE of the items you have secreted away and milk its entertainment value for all it is worth. For our family, the general rule was no more than one secret weapon deployed in a given hour, unless of course there were extenuating circumstances, like a snowed-in flight or an impending toddler implosion, in which case, all bets are off, and I fire away with all available ammunition!

## What About Portable DVD Players?

We are regularly asked HOW we manage to travel so extensively with children without major meltdowns, sibling discord or a mind numbing stream of, "Are we there YET?" and "I'm BORED!" type interactions.

Once, a coworker was SHOCKED to learn that we planned to DRIVE to Central America and back over a four month period, "WHAT are you going to do with your children in the car for FOUR MONTHS?!" she asked, incredulous. My husband smirked, and with characteristic dry humor replied, "Well, a while back, we taught them to read."

We're often asked whether or not we own a portable DVD player and to weigh in on the debate over whether traveling kids need them. **First, let me say, that whether or not a family uses a portable DVD player is a personal decision and there is no "right" or "wrong" way to travel with kids.** If you want one, get it, and use it without guilt. I will, however, tell you why we have chosen not to.

We've been a TV free family for the better part of eight years now. Before that, we had one, but used it infrequently. We chose, quite consciously, to do other things with our time and to preserve our children from the intrusive marketing that is rampant in the American media culture. We did, occasionally, watch movies or rent documentaries as a family and as part of the children's schooling. Since we had not become addicted to it at home, we saw no reason to take it on the road in the form of a portable DVD player.

When we travel, we do so to experience things as a family, for personal growth, for cultural immersion, for the love of the world, for the educational benefit to our kids. If our children are plugged in instead of engaged, they may be quieter, but they also might as well be at home in the living room. Quieter is not our goal.

25

They are missing the experience we are wanting them to have. We saw a boy of about ten sitting on a stone in the Colosseum of Rome playing a hand held gaming device instead of experiencing the richness of his surroundings. How sad.

**Constant entertainment also robs a child of the opportunity to develop contentment and a "happy for what I have" attitude.**

**Instead of learning to amuse himself, create a life of the mind and use his imagination creatively, a DVD player, game boy, or other entertainment system, allows him to effectively "check out" of a situation that might otherwise promote personal growth. He is not learning to entertain himself, he is becoming dependent on outside "amusement" to ensure his happiness.**

What did our kids do, for four months in the car, without a DVD player or other form of electronic entertainment? They read, we listened to books on tape, we played various travel games, like license plate bingo, they competed for prizes (a quarter paid for the first palm tree or cactus of the trip) we counted windmills, we debated, they listened to music, created pod casts to share with the world, wrote stories, drew, made up elaborate games and sometimes, they lost temper with one another... they're kids, after all.

Another disadvantage of using DVD players or portable gaming systems in the car is that it can cause motion sickness in some children. If your child seems to have a chronic problem with nausea, try banning electronics during car rides, and see if it may be the culprit.

I'm not going to tell you whether you should use electronic entertainment devices, or not. Instead, I'm going to challenge you to think through your purpose in travel and your purpose in using, or not, a DVD player or other child distraction box. I encourage you, as parents, to be intentional in the habits you build into your child's character and to begin as you mean to go, in the direction that is right for your family.

## Keri Says:

Our family bans DVDs as well as electronic hand-held games during trips because in our experience they make the kids whiny. When our children are tuned into a false world, they have less patience with the real world, which leads to fights among the siblings. Instead of helping one another, the virtually-minded child looks inward, with the goal pleasing himself rather than being helpful and patient with others.

Think of it this way: in a computer game, the character has a set of tasks, challenges and rewards. If anything gets in the player's way, either virtually (like the rival character), or in reality (such as a loud sibling), the player is frustrated in his attempt to meet the goal. This frustration translates very quickly into the real-world.

This is not to say children should never play computer games, in fact, our children each have them, but the time spent on them is monitored, and when traveling, the gadgets are left at home. Travel requires a team effort, and if a team member is focused solely on meeting his own goals (whether real or imagined), he will not play well with others.

# CHAPTER 2: HEALTHCARE

Staying well on the road is a concern for travelers of all ages, even more so when you have children. Careful planning is necessary to be sure that your child will remain healthy as you travel and to be sure that you are well equipped to deal with any medical emergencies that may arise.

There will be a big difference in the amount, and type, of preparation depending on the length of your trip and where you are planning to go. A two-week vacation to a resort is an entirely different thing than setting out for six months or a year to live in a foreign place.

There is no way for us to cover every contingency in this book. Instead, we'll point you to some good resources and paint some broad brush strokes to get you thinking and planning in the right direction.

*Hannah's "ambulance boat" ride on Lago de Atitlan, Guatemala with a cracked ankle bone*

In general, there are three areas of health care that need to be considered when embarking on a trip with travelers of any age. These are: maintenance health care, destination specific risks and emergency health care. Let's look at these one by one, as each relates to your child.

## Maintenance Health Care

We all know children require a lot of physical care and a lot of healthcare oversight in their first years. Most of us schedule regular doctor visits to monitor the growth and development of our children and to be sure that they are reaching developmental milestones appropriately. Most of us also follow an immunization schedule during the early years to be sure our children are protected from life threatening diseases like polio, Diptheria, Tetanus, Hepatitis and others.

If you plan to travel at any point in your child's life, it is very important to familiarize yourself with the immunization schedule and to schedule the appropriate check ups along the way. If you carry a record of your child's immunization dates, any doctor in any clinic can review what has already been administered and continue with regular treatment.

If you are traveling for any length of time, it is an excellent practice to carry a copy of your child's medical records with you. Maintenance health care is important for any child, but for a child who travels extensively, it's even more important, as your child will be exposed to foods, bacteria, and possibly viruses or other organisms a baby remaining at home would not. This is not necessarily a bad thing, it's just an additional aspect of the reality of parenting on the road that needs to be weighed carefully and wisely managed.

## Destination Specific Risks

We were amused to realize, recently, that our youngest child thinks typhoid and yellow fever vaccinations are part of the usual childhood roundup of shots. For our family, they were. Before we set off to cycle two continents and backpack part of a third, there was (and continues to be) much research on the destination specific risks of the places we intend to visit.

Even seemingly innocuous locations, like the southern coast of Italy, during certain years are home to typhoid outbreaks--and you're not going to want to get anywhere close to the equator without a yellow fever shot. Our kids moan loudly about the bitter anti-malaria pills that we dole out every Sunday morning when we're in Central America, but not taking them is simply not an option for us.

I know there are lots of folks who travel without getting the shots, or taking the bitter pills, and there are arguments on both sides of the issue. It is imperative that you be well researched and well informed as to the increased risks of disease exposure as relates to your specific destinations and make your health related decisions carefully.

I had a friend in high school die of meningitis she picked up on a spring break trip to Brazil. Just two weeks ago a friend's son returned home from a humanitarian mission to the Dominican Republic with a mosquito bite that resulted in a very high fever, infection and hospitalization both in the DR and when he returned home.

Not every health care risk can be reduced. Not every disease can be immunized for (dengue, for example). But many can; and those immunizations that are available, should be carefully considered, as sometimes there is not a second chance. The CDC website has a thorough list of recommended immunizations and precautions to be taken, by country and region. Do your homework and give yourself enough time to allow the doses to become effective in your system before heading out.

Food and Water:

**Some places in the world the food and water can pose a health risk in the form of parasites or bacteria that result in intestinal difficulties. A child who is affected by one of these organisms is at an especially high health risk, as life-threatening dehydration happens quickly in small children.**

Use only bottled water in preparing your child's food and thoroughly disinfect all fruits and vegetables using iodine tablets, grapefruit seed crush extract (GSE) or bleach water before feeding them to your child.

Adhere strictly to the bleach-boil-peel rule (only eat it if you have bleached it, boiled it or peeled it) and you'll minimize the risks significantly. For our family, I bleach even if we're going to peel, as bacteria on the peel can be transferred to the inside of the fruit on the knife you're using.

To use bleach as a disinfectant for fresh fruits and veggies, simply soak the produce in a solution of bleach (1 Tbsp) and water (1 qt./L) for twenty minutes, rinse with purified water and then prepare as you normally would.

To use GSE, use 15 drops of extract per quart of water and soak the veggies for twenty minutes, rinse with purified water and prepare as you normally would. GSE can also be taken internally (5 drops to a glass of water) to cut down on intestinal difficulties while traveling.

## Emergency Health Care

No matter how careful you are, how prepared you are, or how well immunized you are, eventually you're going to have a health care emergency with your child. This is equally true whether you travel or stay home.

When traveling with a child, it is especially important to be prepared for these emergencies, to minimize the trauma and the potential health consequences for everyone. While you can't predict when an emergency will strike, or how bad it will be, there are a few things you can do to prepare:

- Carry the appropriate documents: medical and immunization records, lists of allergies to foods, medicines and environmental factors, lists of medications and vitamins currently being taken.
- Take the appropriate classes: There is no excuse for not being first aid and CPR certified. Our children take the classes by ten years-old, and we review periodically. No parent should be without these skills.
- Do your homework: Make it your first priority to locate the nearest medical center or hospital when you arrive in a new area. Private hospitals are your best bet in 3rd world countries.
- Carry a medical kit: I'm not talking about the $20 basic first aid kit available at the drug store, I'm talking about a REAL medical kit.

The necessity of this was driven home for us on an idyllic tropical evening, camped on the side of a volcano in a little town in the highlands of Guatemala when our middle son, Elisha, who was nine at the time, cut the tip of his finger almost completely off whilst working on some fish.

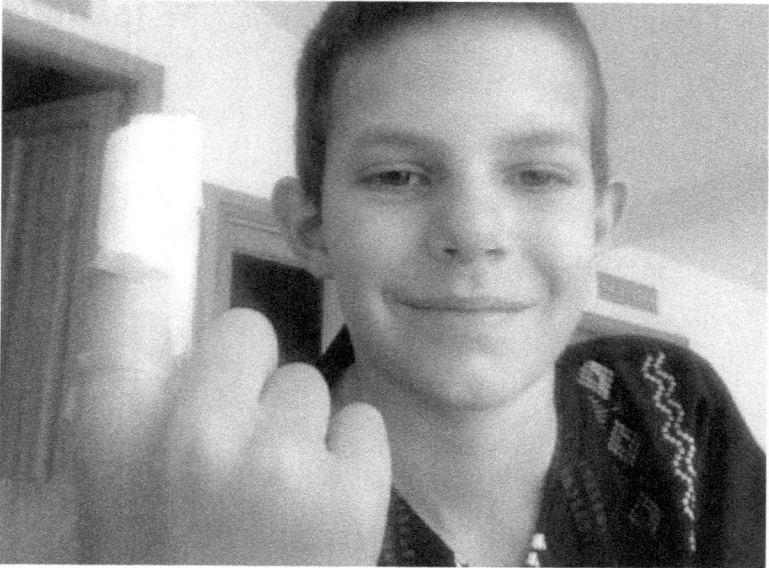

It was our first experience with a third world hospital. It was not confidence inspiring. There was no suture kit in the entire hospital; nor were there butterfly bandages. In the end, what I had in my health kit was better than what the doctors could provide.

They did, however, hook us up with an unidentifiable pain medication: "23 drops every three hours" and an antibiotic to ward off infection. What did I learn? That I needed to add a suture kit to the bag.

What should you have in your medical bag?

Consider the following as "the basics" and build outward from there:

- Bandages of all sizes
- Antibiotic ointments
- Burn treatment
- Blister pads
- Spray pain reliever, like lidocaine
- Tongue depressors

- Tape
- Ankle, wrist and knee braces
- Dental filling replacement pack
- Antibiotic prescription for each family member
- The usual pain meds
- A prescription of serious pain meds
- A suture kit
- Instant ice and heat packs (the chemical gel kind you shake to activate)
- Swabs
- Peroxide
- Alcohol
- Tweezers
- Needle nose pliers
- Butterfly bandages
- Superglue (for major minor cuts)
- Anti-nausea, anti-diarrhea, anti-gas and antacid meds
- For a young child, add infant medications, anti-colic water for an upset tummy and smaller versions of the bandages.

Be sure to ask your doctor for prescriptions of things you're likely to need, like antibiotics and real pain medication, cough medicines, inhalers, or anything you could possible want in a pinch and have a hard time getting overseas. Yes, almost all of these things CAN be found wherever you go... but it minimizes stress in the middle of the night to have them on hand.

## Possibles Kit & The "Hallelujahs"

An emergency health kit is a "must have" for travel with children, but so is an emergency "everything else" kit. My Dad always called this the "possibles kit" because it contained everything else you might possibly need.

- Duct tape
- Permanent markers
- Safety pins
- Velcro straps
- Vinyl and cloth patches
- Sewing supplies
- Scissors
- Waterproof matches
- A lighter
- Fish hooks
- Replacement parts for camp stoves, water filters or bike tires

All of these have all been a part of our possibles kits on various expeditions.

The contents of the kit will vary depending on the type of trip you're taking, where you're going and who's along for the ride, but with a toddler on board there will be certain items you'll want to have that I refer to as the "Hallelujahs."

These are not to be confused with the "Hail Marys" which are what you say when you're so desperate you need one of your Hallelujahs!

Why the Hallelujahs? Because these simple things are an answer to prayer and will make you rejoice :

- Anti-bacterial wipes: We've used these for everything from disinfecting the peels of questionable fruits and veggies in a pinch in third world countries, to cleaning up vomit, to mopping the floors of our tents. **Hallelujah.**

- Ziploc Bags: snack containers, ice packs, the place to pack your emergency clean baby clothes, "waterproofing" for your cell phone on a rainy afternoon, diaper blow-out containment, and what the kids fill with toys for the trip: one ziploc bag, that's all you get. **Hallelujah**.

- Coke, for the Mama... the kind in a can, not the white stuff! We discovered this one, quite by accident, camped outside of Vienna, Austria. We were sitting on our tarp, hot, tired, demoralized on several levels, four months into a year long camping adventure, sipping cold Cokes, the nectar of life, the blood running through the veins of most Americans, at least. He summed it up perfectly for us, our friend Pirate Scott, as he cheerfully tramped by to his tent. "Coke is good for morale! Cheers!" And so it is. Maybe it's not Coke for your family, but find out what it is, and pack it. Mama's morale is at least as important as the kid's comfort when it comes to travel happiness. **Hallelujah**.

## The Miller Boys Recommend:

Bigger kids will get a lot of joy out of creating their own little "possibles kits" to carry in their own bags.

What would my boys recommend you include:

- Waterproofed matches in a screwtop container
- A needle and thread
- Earplugs
- A bouncy ball
- A balloon
- Fish hooks & line
- A knife (Gabe says NOT to take this if you're flying... and you can trust him on that. Yes, he tried.)

## Websites for Traveler's Healthcare:

CDC Traveler's Health Information by country & recommended vaccines

World Nomads Health Insurance

CDC Travel with Infants & Children Page

# CHAPTER 3: TRANSPORTATION

## By Plane

Flying may be exciting when you're in a Piper Cub, but flying in a jet liner is like taking a bus, only without the scenery. Sure, takeoff and landing and the occasional turbulence may get your heart racing, but flying is one mode of transportation that is purely practical—get from A to B as quickly and uneventfully as possible.

If you're paralyzed by the fear of behavioral issues, or mired in the quandary of your pack list, take heart, you're not alone. You can do this! There are a few things every Gypsy Mama should know to make the tedious part of the journey go more smoothly.

### Food:

For Babies: If you're nursing, no problem. If formula is on the menu, bring individual packets—and only as many as you'll need. If you have established a routine, you should know exactly how many packets of formula to bring. Bring two extra if the 'what-ifs' are particularly troublesome. Leave the juice at home. Juice can easily be purchased once you're through security or wait for the complimentary stuff on the airplane.

For Older Kids: Though you want broaden your child's palate, I am not convinced airline food qualifies. Many

airlines now offer special meals for children and infants--
ask about it when you book your tickets. This is one time
when making the extra effort to order the kids' meal is
perfectly reasonable, as it might make your flight go a
touch smoother. Request special meals well ahead of your
travel dates, as some airlines require at least a week
notice.

When bringing your own food: Take into consideration your
child's schedule. Take only as much food as your child
typically consumes during the time you will be flying
(including airport waiting time.) Also take into consideration
quality versus quantity. A few cheese sticks offer more
protein (thus keeping him filled up longer) than an entire
box of cereal. Avoid foods that are sky-high in empty carbs.
Though you do need some carbs for energy, you don't want
your child to have a sudden burst of energy followed by a
complete crash (which usually comes in the form of an
emotional meltdown).

Before we travel, we have a meal that is high in protein and
that has a few carbs.

Our pre-travel menu: Omelets or oatmeal, yogurt, and fruit
for those who can tolerate it. If you have a child who is
prone to motion sickness, as we do, avoid fruit because of
the acidity.

**Child Restraints:**

For Babies: If your baby is traveling in your lap then you
have no need to schlep that carseat. The best bet is to rent
one when you arrive or, at very least, check it with your
baggage.

Use a sling or wrap to secure the child to you. This way,
you'll have your hands free for showing tickets and pulling
out passports. Remember, airlines do not allow a child to
be secured to your body during takeoff and landing. You
may have to undo straps during those times.

If your child is able to sit up on his own, a special seatbelt for lap babies may be available. Check with your airline before you go. By the time your lap baby graduates to child fare, she will be big enough to be secured into a seat with the existing lap belt.

For Toddlers: Your child is no longer a lap baby and now has her own seat. So now you wonder whether or not to bring the carseat. There is debate on this point, but the Gypsy Mamas suggest you don't bring the carseat on the airplane. That's right. Leave it. It's just one more thing to carry, and you're going to rent one if you need it, right?

Car seats do not guarantee your child will sit contentedly during a flight. Instead of hauling more stuff, train him to sit still, secured by the lap belt. Prepare yourself for a lot of gentle but firm direction.

Our toddlers had long legs, which meant they were perfect for kicking the seats in front of them (often by accident). Our solution was to have the child sit crisscross, if he could do so comfortably.

If you feel additional restraint is necessary, consider one of the more portable airline child safety belts, like the CARES Restraint

**Strollers:**

You have enough to deal with simply by traveling with kids. Don't add to your workload by bringing a stroller.

First, there is always a struggle on the jetway with folding and gate checking.

- After your flight, you end up standing in the gangway (usually apologizing) while other passengers try to get past. It is a time waster and a hassle.
- Additionally, many airports are not stroller friendly. Escalators are verboten for strollers. Lifts are tiny (in Europe) and the queues long.

Why bother when you can simply traipse down the steps with the toddler following, or in a sling. This is when you will be glad you spent time playing follow-the-leader at home.

If you insist on taking the stroller, the time to practice folding it is not when hundreds of people are glaring at you.

Practice until you can fold your stroller fluidly at home and time yourself.

- Then try to beat your own record.
- When you think you're fast, do it with one arm tied behind your back.
- Then try it while holding your infant, as may be the case in the airport.

Children do not drain the fun out of travel; the joy-stealer is the unnecessary baggage. If traveling is to be an enjoyable family lifestyle, be courageous and ditch the stroller.

# Practicalities of Flying

Tickets: If your lap baby turns two during your travels, you will be charged by your airline for a separate seat on the return flight. Some airlines do offer child fares. Check with your specific airline to find out the details.

Special Services: Take the time to pre-board. This is not indulgent, but a mercy to other travelers. Pre-boarding allows time for your toddler to walk down the gangway and hop on board. She can move down the aisles (possibly trip and cry) without clogging up the plane's arteries.

Pre-boarding also gives you time to get yourself and the child settled. If you have adhered to the one bag rule, the boarding process will be simple (and the flight attendants will be thankful).

### Links To Infant/Child Travel Policies:

- American Airlines
- British Airways
- Air France
- Cathay Pacific
- Lufthansa
- Air Canada

## The Transportation Security Administration (TSA)

Whether it's because of the business man who forgets to take his laptop out of his bag; the Gucci-bag woman who, judging from the shopping bags slung on her arm, spent way too much time at Harrods; or the beleaguered parents wrestling with their stroller; airport security can be the queue from hell for the unprepared.

When going through security, all kid gear (including slings, wraps, blankets, strollers, or car seats) must be put through the x-ray machine. If it does not fit on the conveyor belt, the gear must be inspected by a TSA security officer.

### TSA Carry-On Policy:

For carry-ons, the TSA has a clear 3-1-1 policy:

- 3.4 oz (100ml) bottles
- 1 quart-sized zip-top bag
- 1 bag per passenger.

However, parents taking infants through security are allowed a "reasonable" amount of formula, breast milk, juice, food, or medication, which can be in containers exceeding 3 ounces and do not have to be contained in zip-top bags. Make sure you tell the security officers you have these items before screening.

Before you get into the line for security, prepare yourself and your belongings. Have all your gear ready to go through the conveyor belt.

Going through screening, you have two options: carry the child or let him walk through on his own:

- If you carry your child through screening, be careful not to touch the sides of the metal detector, as this will trigger the alarm. If for any reason the alarm sounds, you and your child must be searched.
- You will not be allowed to pass the child to anyone in front or behind you during security screening. Also, the security officer is not allowed to hold the child for you.

From the time our children could walk, we opted to have them go through security on their own. We didn't do this for mere fun; it was necessity. On several occasions we had preschoolers, toddlers, and an infant—so, walking independently through airport security was inevitable for the toddlers of our family

## The Method:

- One parent goes through first
- The child goes next (or children, oldest to youngest, one at a time)
- And then the second parent follows

Sound easy? It's not. Your child might flip out and start crying, or worse, make a break for it.

It's imperative to "play" airport security at home before you go.

- Have your child hold his hands together (so he's not tempted to touch the sides of the metal detector)
- Then have him practice walking through a doorway without touching the sides

46

- Make sure to include the reason why you are doing this
- If you are traveling alone with your toddler, teach the child to go through, step to the side, and freeze.

If you prepare at home, and use the less-is-more policy, it will be just as easy for you to go through security screening as it is for the average traveler.

Make the process easier by adhering to the TSA rules and regulations. The TSA website offers specific instructions and videos on how to make the process smoother for you and your child.

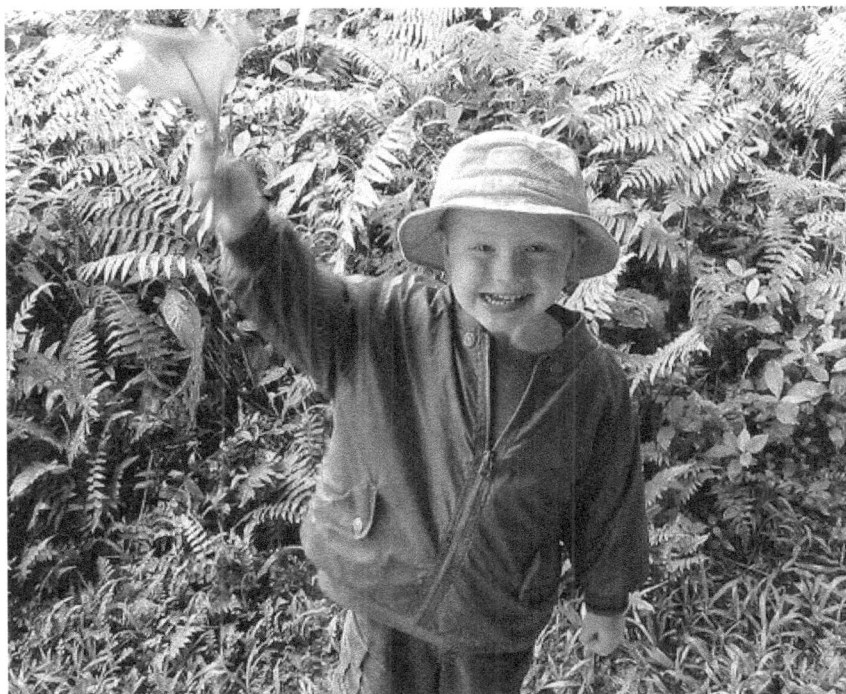

# Jet Lag & Junior: I'm Awake in Hawaii at 3 a.m.

I hate jet lag, and I'm an adult. It drives me crazy to wake up before dawn the first morning I find myself on the west coast and to try to go to sleep at what feels like mid-afternoon my first night in the UK. With kids, it's that much worse. I'm awake in Hawaii at 3 a.m. and there are two little kids staring at me over the edge of the bed. They're awake too. So what do we do? Take a midnight stroll on the sand!

There are all manner of suggested strategies for minimizing jet lag or avoiding it altogether, from taking a certain vitamin regimen to sunlight therapy, to switching the clocks slowly at home until you're on the new schedule before you leave. Personally, I don't think any of them work.

Jet lag is simply one of the travel evils that must be endured and it's as hard on toddlers as it is on the Mama.

**A few tips that MIGHT help... no promises:**

- Stay up: Go to bed no earlier and no later in the new time zone than you would have at home, that goes for the kiddies too.
- Get fresh air: Something about the fresh air (perhaps the sunlight?) does seem to help reorient the system.
- Drink lots of water: Staying properly hydrated helps a body feel its best, no matter the time zone. Keep the kids drinking too!
- Maintain a consistent schedule for your toddler: The first three days when you're recovering from jet lag is the time for routine and consistency, not wild sightseeing from dawn 'til dusk.
- Get up: If everyone's awake and there's clearly no going back to sleep, make an adventure of it, and have some fun. Laying in bed is miserable when you're a little kid.
- Pack your sense of humor.

## By Train

Traveling by rail in Europe is a fantastic option for families. Long distance rail, in particular, is an excellent way to get from A to B and beyond.

On Deutschebahn, in Germany, children under age 14 ride for free with parents. By speaking with DB representatives, you can book travel in a family cabin on the ICE trains.

If you will be traveling on weekends, during heavy commuter traffic, or on holidays, pay the extra fee to reserve seats in advance, or else you may find yourself standing for the duration of travel.

Though children are free, they must be listed on the ticket for long-distance trains.

Note: trains in countries outside of the UK, Austria and Germany may not run like clockwork. Make sure you have a flexible fare (or a flexible schedule) if traveling outside of these regions.

Traveling by rail outside of Europe can be more challenging.

There are comparatively few rail routes in North America

- The quality of service will vary greatly across Asia
- Very little rail travel exists in Africa

It is important to do your research and prepare for the unique challenges of rail travel that will meet you in various countries.

## Links to Rail Companies By Country:

- Germany
- United Kingdom
- Italy
- France
- USA
- Canada

## By Metro:

Most major cities in Europe, and abroad, have metro service.

The metro in most cities is the easiest and most economical way to travel to the major sights on your itinerary. Upon arrival in your city of choice, speak with a ticket agent to decide which fare is best for your family.

- In Berlin, the "tageskarte" allows for one day travel within the central city for 2 adults and up to 4 children.
- London's underground allows children up to age 12 to travel free with parents.
- In NYC Up to three children 44 inches tall and under ride for free on subways and local buses when accompanied by a fare paying adult.

Strollers & Trains Don't Mix!

**If traveling by train or metro with a toddler, it is vital to leave the stroller behind. If you are not comfortable with your toddler walking hand-in-hand, either carry him or use a sling.**

While it is possible to take your stroller in the metro, it makes the trip more difficult than it need be (if you've ever been to Boston you KNOW what we mean!) Hands-free is the best way to go.

Leaving the stroller behind also makes it easy to navigate the steep escalators and stairs in most metros. Lifts can be difficult to find and maneuver. Also, the more stuff you have to distract you, the more vulnerable you are to pickpockets and thieves.

**Train Proof Your Kids!**

In the metro station: teach him to "mind the gap" by hopping or making a big step over the space between the platform and the train. Grab the nearest open seat (this process may remind you of musical chairs). If you can't get a seat, teach your child to hold onto the pole in the middle, or sit cross-legged between your feet.

Practice at home: by "gluing" his hands. Make a gesture as if you are pasting his fingers and palms and have him "stick" them to things. At a park, the fireman's pole is perfect. Merry-go-rounds also give you something to hold onto and adequate motion. But, you can pretend to stick his hands to other items too, such as shopping carts or balustrades. Create a key word or phrase when you play (such as "you're stuck"), so you can give the simple command, and he will know what to do.

## By Taxi

In most places, taxis and other forms of public transportation are exempt from seat belt laws.

This means legally, a child under age three is allowed to ride on a parent's lap. Over age three, the existing belts in the taxi can be used.

Some cab companies and private shuttle services offer child safety seats. If you know your itinerary and call ahead, you can arrange this.

There is a lot of debate over child safety and cab rides. Think about your destination and how the locals transport their children, the safety concerns, weigh the risks and make an informed decision for your family.

*Miller kids getting in a tuk-tuk taxi in Guatemala*

# CHAPTER 4: ACCOMMODATION OPTIONS

**Where should we stay?**

If you are going to a major city, it can be wonderful to stay near the sights at the top of your "must-see" list. With kids, it can be a glorious thing to roll out of bed, have breakfast, and get right your destination without a lot of extra travel time.

But if downtown is out of your price range, look further afield. Most major cities are well-connected to the city center by metro. If you stay in an outlying zone, look for something near a metro stop.

There are many benefits of staying outside the city center: cheaper prices for lodging, supermarkets nearby, and more options for eating out with the locals, rather than with the tourists.

## At a Hotel

If you are accustomed to the super-sized hotel rooms of America, brace yourself for the rest of the world, where a triple is considered a 'family room.'

53

Check your hotel's policy regarding children. Some hotels may be able to accommodate a larger family in rooms not necessarily listed on the website. Contact the hotel directly to find out.

If traveling in Europe, be aware that older buildings often do not have standard-sized rooms.

A double on the third floor of your Biedermeier hotel may be smaller than a double on the first floor

- Ask to see the room before you're obligated
- They may have the same room type with a little more space: space you will certainly need with children along.

Anywhere in the Third World, the rule of thumb is simple:

- Consult other travelers
- ALWAYS ask to see the room (check the water, toilet, electricity, AC, etc. before you pay)

## At a Holiday Apartment

FeWo, holiday flat, self-catering apartment, camera, pension: whatever word you use, holiday apartments can be the best way to go for a traveling family.

Most holiday apartments are equipped with a full kitchen (including pots, pans, and utensils) and bath. Holiday apartments are available in every place I've ever wanted to travel, and are less expensive than hotels. You can rent directly from owners or from apartment agencies.

Before booking a holiday apartment, look at the pictures, and then mentally add ten years to it. Unless you are rich, the apartment will never be quite what it seems in the photos. The bathrooms will be smaller. Some light fixtures will be nothing more than bare, hanging wires. The stairs will be creaky. But if you can look past all that, a holiday apartment can be the perfect place for families.

**Things to ask before letting a holiday apartment:**

**Are you the owner?** I have found renting directly from owners to be a better experience. Owners care about their apartments, know a lot about the area, and usually have more time to answer your questions. Agencies generally rush.

**What type of security does the building have?** Even if you have done your homework on areas of town, you can never quite know what a neighborhood is like until you get there. One block may be luxury high-rises, the next a slum.

**Are the owners or previous tenants smokers?** There's nothing worse than being a non-smoker who has doled out a chunk of the budget to find an apartment that smells like an ashtray. If cigarette smoke is something that bothers you, or if you are allergic, make sure you ask before you go. There are no refunds for unasked questions.

**Is the building undergoing renovations?** The historic building you've booked the family in may look lovely online, but there may be scaffolding covering that art nouveau facade. Unless you want to rise and shine to the sounds of the hammer every morning, this one is important.

**Is there construction on the street?** If you have children who nap, you may not want to rent a place where jackhammers are heard all day. Furthermore, construction on the street can make your holiday apartment difficult to get to and to find. Bag drags are difficult enough in new cities, without the added challenges of closed roads and detours.

**Is there a supermarket nearby?** Holiday apartments most often do not come with amenities such as soap, shampoo, or even (to my horrible surprise once) toilet paper. Furthermore, if you plan on making use of the kitchen (which you have already perused to see what you're lacking) a supermarket is a necessity. If you are like our family and a food allergy is a problem, having a supermarket nearby is a lifesaver.

**Where is the closest metro, bus, or taxi stand?** If you opted out of the city center, public transportation should be close enough to walk easily to. Caution: many neighborhoods near train stations are unsavory. Do your homework before you book lodging! Websites such as tripadvisor are helpful; or look at comments guests have left for hotels in that neighborhood to get a sense of the place.

**Can you accommodate children?** Sometimes apartment owners will give you a price break if they know you are traveling with children (as opposed to three adult couples splitting the entire cost). Ask if there is a discount for families. Also, take a good look at the pictures on the website. Does the apartment have a lot of glass tables and knick-knacks? You may opt for something that looks a little more durable.

**Does it have WiFi?** Even if this is not a deal-breaker, sometimes owners forget to tell you, even if they have it. If you know ahead of time WiFi is available, you can make sure you get the security code before the owner drops off the keys and heads out the door.

**What floor is it on?** If it's been a few years since you lived in an apartment, this might be a good question for you to ask. If you are on the top floor, ask if there's a lift, or you will be doing some major stair-stepping (which might be difficult for your children). If you're on the bottom floor, you may be listening to every move your upstairs neighbors make. If noise from neighbors is something that bothers you (especially if you pay several hundred dollars for the apartment), make sure to ask about the building.

**Should I be so picky?** If you want to live with the locals, then issues such as smoking, sounds of neighbors, and what floor the apartment is on may not be so important. But if you are in a major metropolitan city to tour the museums, you may want to maintain certain levels of comfort. If this is your first excursion with your toddler, then traveling itself will be the challenge, so you should make your home base as comfortable as possible.

**Useful Resources for Holiday Apartments:**

http://www.holidaylettings.co.uk/

http://www.homeaway.com/

Thanksgiving dinner in apartment in Tunisia

Home rented in Guatemala

## Hostels

If hotels are too pricey and you aren't interested in, or can't find, an apartment or home rental, you should consider staying at a Youth Hostel.

We were surprised to find that hostels can be extremely family friendly. Yes, the primary type of traveler found in a hostel is a twenty-something gap year adventurer with a backpack, but you'll also find grandparents, other families with kids, business professionals and more.

One of the primary reasons we travel is to expose our kids to the people of the world and hostel stays are an excellent way to do that.

Invariably the collection of travelers you'll find in the hostel common room are an interesting and diverse lot. Our kids have spent many a pleasant evening swapping travel stories with young people twice their age, knitting quietly next to a grandma who's knitting too, or playing loud games of pool or soccer with partially inebriated college kids. More than once Ezra has been carried through a hostel on some young man's shoulders, the chosen mascot of the hostel youth for the duration of our stay.

Many hostels now offer a larger "family room" option for people traveling with children. Alternately, if your family is a nice big one (like ours!) you can often fill out an entire six bed dorm room... which means that you just scored yourself a private room (like at a hotel!) for a fraction of the price! That's almost reason enough to have a couple more kids, don't you think?

We look at hostels as a "culturally broadening experience" and we seek to stay in them as often as possible. Hands-down, our BEST hostel experiences have been in New Orleans at Mardi Gras, and on Martha's Vineyard during a hurricane... oh... and the one in Amsterdam was pretty cool too... actually, we love them all!

Well... except that ONE in Antigua that sold Mama's bed out from under her when she was traveling alone... and she had to SHARE... with a STRANGER... that one's not our favorite!

Make sure you ask in advance about their policy regarding children and inquire after the amenities that are offered.

# Camping

Camping with kids is a blast! It's cheap, it's adventurous, and it's a learning experience. If you haven't camped since you were a kid, now is the time to dive back in. Find a local campground (close enough to home to bail out if it all goes wrong) and sleep in a tent, cook food over an open fire, gorge yourselves on marshmallows and sing hokey songs while you do it.

Once you've got your feet wet locally and have enthusiastic campers, I heartily recommend branching out and camping longer term. When we cycled Europe and Tunisia, we camped a lot of the time. It was a great way to meet locals and other travelers. We've camped our way through Central America, as well as the USA and Canada and our kids STILL love it.

What will make your camping adventures a success instead of a dismal failures: the right gear. If you plan to camp "for a living" like we do, or even camp more than the odd weekend in summer, make the investment in proper camping gear. Cheap tents leak. Cheap sleeping bags get cold and matted. Smaller is almost always better. Quality is worth paying for.

Our personal pick for tents beyond compare is the Hilleberg company. They are hell AND high water proof, they can be set up by a six year old with a rock to pound stakes with, and their customer service is absolutely first rate.

Beyond tents and more flexible are camping hammocks. We have six made by Hennessy and have spent many a dry night hanging in the rain forest in them. Ezra says to tell you the howler monkeys and jaguars sounded scary in the dark!

Free-camping in Germany

Hammocks under bungalow at Tikal

# Camping With Toddlers

The toddler years are wonderful years to introduce your little person to the joys of camping! What better way to teach flexibility than to sleep out of doors, in a tent, on the ground and introduce the idea that marshmallows are a bedtime snack?

Your toddler may show some initial worry about the darkness, a sleeping bag instead of his comfy bed, or the unusual sounds that surround a tent when camping. You can overcome these with a positive attitude and consideration.

Our toddlers have loved camping because of the treats that inevitably come with a night in the tent in our family. Namely, a much longer story-time as we read aloud until little eyes close completely, and snuggling down in between Dad and Mom in the sleeping bag, a privileged sleeping spot that is rarely won by toddlers at home (unless they're sick elves!)

Everything that would be ho-hum in the house is an adventure out of doors:

- Cooking: over a fire instead of a stove
- Eating: on the ground instead of in a highchair
- Washing up: in a bucket or riverbed instead of in the dishwasher
- Bath time: in a camp shower (if you're lucky!) or a lake instead of a tub

Little children will dig in to these everyday adventures with gusto if you encourage them to help and work alongside you.

If you wait to introduce camping until you have a moody eleven year old, it might be a hard sell. If you take your toddlers camping you'll have eleven year olds who love it, in spite of the "uncool" factor!

A few tips for making camping with toddlers a success:

Child sized gear. Maria Montessori had so much right in her assessment of children wanting to do real tasks and serious work as part of their learning. Her admonition to provide children with real tools, sized appropriately, is sage wisdom for any parent. If your toddler has his own little mess kit, a tiny sleeping bag, a head lamp for chasing fireflies in the darkness or trekking to the bath house before bedtime he will rise to the occasion and be proud of his "real camper" status.

In addition to gearing up properly, start small. A child's first camping trip should not be a three day hike into the back country. The backyard is a good place for the first night in a tent. That way if very real fears overwhelm a little person his bed and comfort items are a short walk away. When the backyard is conquered move on to a weekend at a nearby campground. Slowly work your way out from there.

We've taken babies as young as four weeks camping and by the time our youngest was five we sold his whole house out from under him and moved him into a tent full time for an entire year.

He would tell you that he sleeps better in a tent than anywhere else, and he does.

# CHAPTER 5: PREPARING TO TRAVEL

## Physical & Mental Demands of Traveling With Children

Traveling with children requires attention to the 7 P's, flexibility and patience. If you prepare for the worst and hope for the best you'll likely have a wonderful experience.

It is important to think ahead about how you will deal with the difficulties that may arise and prepare yourself, mentally and physically, for the challenge.

After you have a few trips under your belt, and you've developed your own travel routines and some confidence, you'll find that traveling with children is very doable, and can even be a lot of fun.

## Flexibility

It's been mentioned before but bears repeating: Flexibility is key when traveling with children of any age, babies especially.

The parents who tend to be most stressed on the road are the parents who are most bound to their preconceived notions.

The children who seem to fight the hardest against those parents are often the ones who are forced outside of their comfort zones too quickly.

Some items on the itinerary are hard dates: planes wait for no man, nor do departing ocean ferries. However, so many of our "deadlines" are self imposed and could easily be flexed a little to accommodate the needs of the littlest travelers.

A wise parent will take into account her child's routine at home when planning the travel schedule. Babies who are most cheerful in the morning will do better at a museum before lunch. Little ones who nap all afternoon might do better on a long plane trip during those hours of the day.

For years we made the 1100 mile drive to Grammy's house overnight because tucking the babies into their car seats at bedtime and waking up on the ferry for breakfast was the path of least resistance for them.

Travel is disruptive to everyone. Instead of pushing ahead with a predetermined agenda, take a step back, reevaluate your goals and expectations, and plan around your child's preexisting routine.

Travel with children opens all sorts of doors to the world you didn't notice before, and it closes others, for a little while at least.

Pick and choose, because you can't do it all.

- Make your plans, breathe deeply, and expect the unexpected.
- Be flexible, and everyone will have more fun.

## In Preparation For The Big Travel Day

For many families the most stressful part of the trip is the first big day of travel to a destination, or the last big day of travel home. If you can structure for success for these two big days you'll get your trip off on the right foot and arrive home peacefully.

Here are a few suggestions of ways that you can make a big day of travel easier on everyone:

- Parents get enough sleep (do NOT stay up until 2 a.m. packing!)
- Children get enough sleep (well rested kids are happier kids!)
- Eat a solid breakfast (including adequate carbs and protein)
- Avoid the need to rush (this only adds stress for everyone)
- Decide ahead of time to remain cheerful & calm no matter what happens

## Physical Preparation

Traveling with children requires pushing, pulling, lifting, and bending—and that's just when you're packing for the trip.

To make your travels as smooth as possible, invest time in your physical health. If you are a runner, schedule time for runs in the weeks prior to travel. If step-aerobics are your cup of tea, get back into it as soon as possible after your children are born.

With a newborn or toddlers, you may not have time (or inclination) to go to the gym. So, when it's okay with your doctor, begin by doing simple exercises at home.

Work your triceps with soup cans (the big ones, not the little ones).

- Bicep curl the baby (carefully, of course).
- Do squats while holding the baby, rather than falling asleep in the rocking chair.

- Walk as much as possible.
- Simple, old-school calisthenics (such as jumping-jacks, push-ups and sit-ups) boast great results for a cheap price.
- Resistance bands are also a great way to improve muscle tone.

The more muscle tone you have, the easier it will be to strap the baby to you and explore new places. Dedicating ten minutes, three times a day can have you feeling stronger in no time.

## Mental Preparation

A new dimension is added to the mix when you travel with your children. During travel, your attention will be fixed upon meeting your child's needs, while being considerate of your fellow passengers.

This is can be mentally exhausting. When you exercise, you are not only preparing your body for the practicalities of travel, but you are preparing yourself mentally as well. Relieving stress through physical exertion will help you to remain calm, even when the kids don't share your agenda for tranquil travel.

You can train your body to relax by using a simple association technique. Whether you meditate, pray, or run to balance your mental health, you can use physical cues to relax your body and mind.

Practice using a physical cue, such as pressing your fingertips together, while you are in a relaxed state. With enough training, your body will use that physical touch to relax the body.

You will react much differently to challenges if you are relaxed, calm, and clear-headed.

## Passports & Visas

If you are traveling outside of your country of origin your child is going to need a passport and perhaps a visa.

Children are subject to the same requirements as adults when traveling internationally. In some countries, like the United States and Canada, children are required to have their own passports.

In other countries, like Germany, children are simply added on to their parent or guardian's passport. It is very important to look into the passport and visa requirements for children, both in your home country and in your destination country, well in advance of your trip. Getting a passport or visa can take several months depending on where you are going.

In the United States, children must have their own passports. Things to remember:

- Both parents must be with the child during application
- The child must have a social security card before applying
- The child must have a certified birth certificate or (if born outside the US) a consular report of birth abroad
- Parents must have evidence of their relationship to the child such as a US birth certificate with both parents' names; a foreign birth certificate with both parents names (with English translation); a report of birth abroad with both parents' names; or adoption degree with both parents' names
- Parents must have valid identification such as a US passport, naturalization certificate, drivers license, military ID, or Government ID
- A photocopy of each ID will be submitted with the application

- Bring two identical 2 x 2 inch color photos of the child, taken within the past 6 months
- If you, the parent, are applying for your first passport, you will additionally need your birth certificate and marriage certificate (if your name has changed).

In the UK, children must have their own passports.

**Things to remember:**

- The requirements for the passport photo are very strict, rather than do it yourself in a photo booth, go to a photo print shop which offers a digital photography service — it's more cost effective if multiple shots are needed to get it right.
- The child must have a birth certificate or certified copy — make sure you get a couple of additional copies when you register the birth of your child.
- It's worth paying for the Post Office's passport application checking service, especially if you're on a deadline; it will prevent delays and ensure there are no problems with your application.

## For More Specific Guidelines on Passport Applications & to Download the Forms:

- For the USA
- For the UK
- For Canada

## What to Wear

Two words: **What's comfortable.**

Travel is easiest when you are physically comfortable. A long day in transit with a child will be easier when you are both wearing something you love.

There is no need to sacrifice fashion for comfort and comfort does not have to mean your old ratty sweats that you clean house in. However, give some thought to your travel wardrobe to balance fashion with comfort and functionality. Choose fabrics that do not easily wrinkle and can be spot cleaned in a flash when a feeding doesn't go as you'd hoped.

There are several great sources of travel clothing that might be worth checking into. If you plan to travel a lot with your child then in it might be worth investing in a few well chosen, travel hardy, pieces to add to your wardrobe.

Consider the following as suggestions for what to wear on your long travel days:

- A knee length microfiber dress that has a crisscross front (for ease of nursing) to blend style with comfort and functionality
- Yoga pants (stretch pants) with a tank top shell and a light weight long sleeved shirt
- Solid, comfortable shoes: leave the heels at home
- Socks, for when you want to slide your shoes off and be comfy
- One piece jumper for baby, the kind that snaps or zips up the front for easy access for diapering and maximum comfort
- A hat for baby, sometimes trains and planes can be chilly

## Haircare

High-maintenance hairstyles are OUT when it comes to traveling with kids. Straightening, styling, curling and blowdrying all require special paraphernalia that could take an entire bag of its own. Remember the big, round cosmetic bag your grandmother took with her on cruises, which perfectly matched the five other pieces of her luggage set? That kind of decadence is not going to fly with the Gypsy Mama.

But it doesn't mean you have to travel the world with hair that would frighten small children.

Find a style that suits you, whether long or short, that doesn't require much more than a brush. If your hair is wavy enough to be frizzy, but not frizzy enough to be curly (like mine), a little gel, a simple headband and clip will do.

**Another gypsy mama secret**--invest in a good travel hat! With a hat you love, you'll never have a bad hair day on the road.

## Sources for Travel Clothing

Athleta: Not just travel clothing, but clothing perfect for travel. Most of Jenn's clothes come from here!

Ex Officio: Not cheap, but high quality and very reliable.

REI: The Miller's favorite source for family travel gear, from clothes to Keens, to baby backpacks and more. One stop shopping and a 100% guarantee.

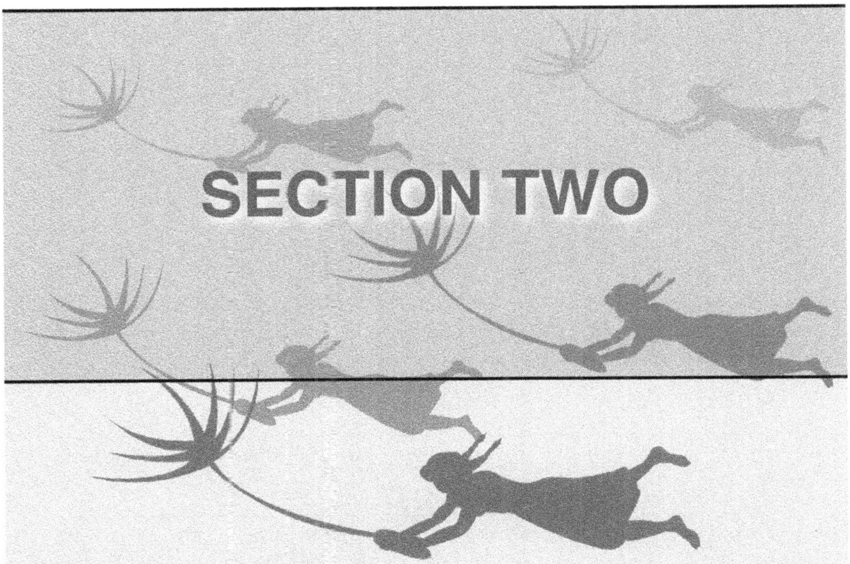

# SECTION TWO

# TRAVEL WITH BABIES

# CHAPTER 6: INTRO TO BABY TRAVEL

## Why Travel with Baby?

You may find yourself questioning your own sanity as you dive into the process to travel with baby. It's not as if, when you lift her to your shoulder for a burp, she will whisper, "Yes, Mother, the mosaics in St. Peter's are truly spectacular."

Why travel with baby when she won't remember anything?

Take a good look at that tiny human being in your arms. At this moment, most of your infant's 100 billion neurons have not yet formed networks. These neural networks, or connections between neurons, are constructed through your baby's interaction with the world around her.

Neural networks form the basis for emotion, language, motor skills, and relationships. For example, during attachment bonding, neural pathways are established which create a sense of security in the child towards her caregiver. This sense of trust allows the baby, as she grows, to confidently explore her world.

Similarly, exposing your baby to a variety of travel scenarios develops neural pathways, which will allow her to more easily navigate the rich world in which she lives.

The reason you travel with baby is not so she can remember the sunset from the Eifel Tower, but so her brain can absorb the sights, sounds, smells, and flavors of cultures deliciously different from her own.

Your infant's brain is constantly taking in and organizing information. The neural networks create a programming of sorts—think of it as wiring the brain for future function.

Exposing the child to travel at an early age can better prepare her to cope with the stress of travel. It helps your baby gain her sea legs, figuratively and literally.

Later, while other parents are figuring out ways to strap down their terrible toddler, your child will have already formed neural networks which allow her to easily process what is going on around her (and not act out in a stress-induced tizzy).

Simply put, your child, whether she is cognizant of it or not, can travel with less stress than other children because she has already "been there, done that."

The more experience your baby has traveling, the more equipped she will be to travel well.

On the flip side, any networks not used in the child's brain are "pruned," or literally cut off. Which simply means, one happy trip to grandma's may not be enough to keep the neural pathways active.

If your ultimate goal is for your child to be a good traveler, then make the effort to travel as much as possible while the baby is young. Even if a nomadic lifestyle isn't your immediate goal, the neural pathways set in infancy will reap huge benefits if travel is in your future.

Stress is a reaction; one that has ramifications chemically. When under stress, the brain produces Cortisol. High levels of this chemical can cause brain cells to wither, which in turn impairs the neural network.

Your baby picks up on your cues: if you are stressed, she will be stressed as well. The best ways to avoid stress are to:

Practice traveling (if it is new to you)

- Exercise or meditate in the weeks prior to travel (and during travel, if you can)
- Practice minimalism when it comes to baby gear

Infancy is the easiest time in a child's life in which to travel. Make the most of it. When your child hits the toddler years, you will be glad you made the effort.

# The Challenges of Traveling With Baby

We have good news for you! Babyhood is, most definitely, the easiest stage of life for traveling with children! That does NOT mean it's always a walk in the park, or that a diaper won't explode at the worst possible moment, or that your fears of six straight hours of a howling baby on a flight are to be minimized.

Traveling with a baby requires real planning, and equal parts patience and flexibility.

However, because this stage is as easy as it's going to get, it makes a GREAT time to get started, the earlier the better. The sooner you and baby make regular travel a part of your routine, the more flexible you will both become and the easier it will get, for both of you.

The chapters in this section are all about managing the challenges, minimizing the potential for disaster and maximizing tranquility and enjoyment for everyone involved.

My babies actually loved to travel, and were quite excited by the sight of an airplane porthole by the time they were old enough to stand on my lap and look out.

Whether your goal is to Grandma's and back over two weeks, or around the world over a year, we can help you make your dream a reality!

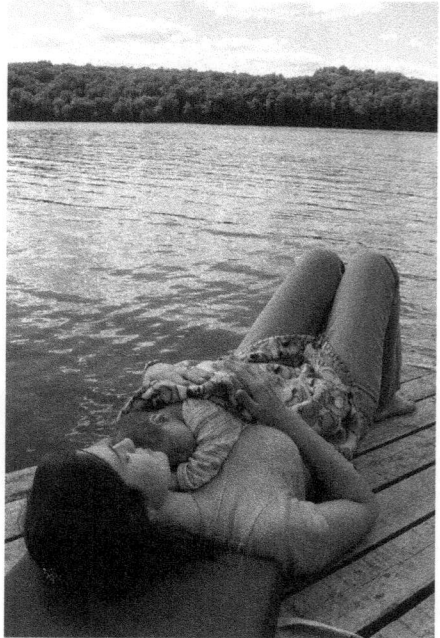

80

# CHAPTER 7: IT ALL STARTS AT HOME!

## Pre-travel Preparation

Remember Uncle Dick's Seven P's? *(Proper Prior Planning Prevents Piss Poor Performance)* This is where the rubber meets the road!

Everyone from MD's to Aunties agree that in child-rearing, routine is important. But what the experts don't tell you is flexibility can become part of your routine.

That's right: routine and flexibility are not mutually exclusive.

Routine does not mean your child eats chicken nuggets for every meal and only sleeps in his race car bed.

Routine is a simple structure of normal living habits.

For infants, it usually looks something like this: sleep, wake, eat.

Routine is what you do; flexibility is how you do it.

If you work to establish flexibility and a routine at home, you'll find taking your baby on the road a much more enjoyable experience, for both of you, as you'll be better prepared to anticipate your baby's needs.

## On Schedules & Infants

What happens to the scheduled baby, for example, if instead of snoozing contentedly in her bassinet at 9 pm, the baby is wide-eyed going through the metal detector at airport security? You may think schedules are too rigid to allow travel flexibility--that by not scheduling, you can more easily placate the baby.

When you use a simple schedule, your infant learns the important differences between play time, sleep time, and feeding time.

As with any area regarding infants, everyone has advice on scheduling: from anti-scheduling rebels who toss the clock out the window, to regime-like fanatics who literally set their alarms. What I've discovered is a happy middle ground, entirely suitable and adjustable for travel:

**The Flex-Schedule**

The flex-schedule begins in the first eight weeks of your infant's life. This is the time to establish a solid home routine. The two main goals of the first 8 to 12 weeks are to get your infant to fall asleep unassisted (without a bottle or without being held) and to sleep through the night. Some babies take a little longer than others, but once these two initial goals are met, life gets easier for everyone.

The Home Routine: Feed, Awake, Sleep, Repeat

## Feeding

When you bring the baby home from the hospital and sit in your rocker for the first time to nurse, glance at the clock. 2 ½ to 3 hours later, you will be feeding the baby again. If the baby cries after only one hour, don't immediately reach for the bottle. See if something else might be wrong.

Unless your infant is showing definite signs of hunger, try to postpone feeding again until the 2 ½ hour mark. When babies eat more frequently (say every 1 ½ hours like my firstborn), they learn to snack. Soon, feeding turns into pacifying rather than nourishment.

For the nursing mom, if you are able to wait 2 ½ hours before feeding, your milk will be superior in quality and quantity, thereby completely satisfying the baby. Thus, the baby's routine can quickly be established.

Be aware, sometimes babies go through growth spurts where they will feed several times within a few hours. This is normal, and the child should always be fed when real signs of hunger are present. These growth spurts should only disrupt the routine for a couple of days. Once the baby is through it, she should settle back down into her routine.

If you are concerned your child is not eating enough, look for the following warning signs: fewer than 6-8 wet diapers a day; irregular bowel movements; constant sleepiness; little interest in feeding; or lack of proper weight gain and consult your healthcare provider immediately.

## Awake Time

Feed the baby when she wakes, not as she is falling asleep. The only caveat to this rule is nighttime feeding. During normal night hours, the baby should eat then be put right back to sleep. During the day, however, feed the baby when she wakes, and then try to keep her awake for a little while. You don't have to do a song and dance to entertain her for wake time. But something as simple as changing her diaper or giving her a bath will keep her awake long enough to establish the routine.

Newborns sleep a lot, but by keeping her awake for a few minutes after feeding, she will begin to learn that feeding is not part of sleeping. By doing this, you are teaching her to fall asleep on her own. This is invaluable when traveling, when consoling or comfort feeding is much more difficult.

## Sleep Time

Your little angel looks lovely when she falls asleep in your arms. You carry her gently to her room, lay her in bed, and then tiptoe away, hoping not to step on any loud toys on your way out. This scenario loses its beauty when your child is two, or three, or five.

It's exhausting feeding the baby round-the-clock, but when she also depends upon you to fall asleep, you'll be on the ragged edge after three months. You may look forward to traveling in the early weeks because the baby will constantly be in your arms, and thus happy. But when she's fighting sleep at nine months because she'd rather be playing with the seat tray in front of her, you have a problem on your hands.

Help your child learn to fall asleep on her own. If your baby has been fed, diapered, and had the appropriate wake time, it is time for sleep. Very simply, lay her in her bed (in a calm, quiet place) and let her cry a little if she needs to.

Do be aware, extensive crying can be a sign something is wrong. Do not neglect your child. But don't be so quick to pick her up every time she fusses. She could be merely settling herself down for a rest, which is disturbed when you enter the picture.

My youngest child had "fussy time" every night from 9 to 10 pm when she was a baby. The only thing I could do was to put her in her bassinet and let her cry. She wasn't hungry, dirty, uncomfortable, or sick; it was simply her way of blowing off steam before bedtime. I put in my earplugs (to take the edge off) and stayed close by to monitor her. It was difficult, to say the least, but her fussy time (I liked to think of it as baby exercise) did not last long. After two weeks, she was going to sleep at night without a fuss. At six weeks old, she dropped her 3 am feeding.

You might object and say my baby was an exception. But my third-born was sleeping through the night by 8 weeks because I took the time to schedule. Even though I was not a strict scheduler with my second child, she still slept through the night by 12 weeks.

Before you wonder if this is merely a genetic fluke (that somehow my children were 'born' good sleepers), I have to make it clear that my oldest child had no schedule as an infant. I couldn't bear to hear him cry, which was why I was still giving him a bottle to put him to sleep when he was nine months old (and hoping he would not wake on the treacherous journey from the living room to the nursery).

Establishing a "firm" home routine does not mean you live by the clock. The clock is a road sign not a landmark. It gives you a general idea of what is coming next; it does not decide when you get there. Over time, her schedule will change. Your child's wake time will turn to play time (where she's smiling at you and grabbing your earrings). The wake time will be longer, the feedings will be further apart, and the nap time will decrease.

If you are traveling during the first eight weeks of your child's life, try to maintain the eat, wake, sleep pattern, and avoid comfort feeding. Arrange your travel time so it meshes with your infant's natural habits. If she sleeps long periods of time at night, that is the time to be stuck on an airplane with her. If she has fussy time from 8 to 9, avoid traveling during those hours. If she tends, like mine, to cry before bedtime no matter what you do, arrange lodging accordingly.

## Flex-Routine and Time Zone Travel

Having established a pattern of living habits during the first few weeks of her life, you and your child know how day-to-day events should play out. Your child trusts you will feed her at the appropriate times. And you will be able to anticipate your child's needs. You will also be better equipped to discern what is troubling her. You will know the difference between her hungry cry, a cry of pain, and her sleepy cry; without a routine in place, telling the difference can be trickier!

There are many things out of your control during travel (such as flight delays or mass transit strikes). Don't let your infant's schedule be one of those unknowns. Knowing what to expect will also help you in packing, as you'll be able to better predict your baby's physical needs.

A solid routine is invaluable when crossing time zones with your baby. If her schedule is typical, it will look like this: baby wakes up and eats; she has play time; she falls asleep.

When traveling, adhere to the pattern, but allow baby to dictate the time shift. My own personal rule is: when traveling, never wake a sleeping baby.

If she normally naps for 1 hour and has already slept 2 on your eight-hour flight, don't wake her. If you wake her early, you may be robbing her body of the adequate rest it requires. The stress of travel can be hard, even in an infant's life. Go with her biorhythms and let her sleep. Plus, a sleepy baby is a grumpy baby. Do not willingly create fussiness in your child because you are still in a different time zone. All bets are off when you're in the air.

However, when your baby DOES wake, stick to the established pattern. Feed her, let her have wake time, then pray she goes back to sleep. Don't become stuck in a time zone you are no longer in. Flights are a sort of twilight zone for schedulers. Even hard and fast rules are tweaked on long journeys.

**When you land**

Keep the pattern the same, but slowly adjust to fit the new daylight hours. If your baby is wide awake in the middle of the night, feed her then put her back to sleep as you would normally.

If she gets her days and nights confused, try keeping her awake more during the day. Don't fall into the trap of entertaining her in the middle of the night, or resort to comfort feeding just to keep her quiet. If she has learned to fall asleep on her own, you should be able to leave her in her crib at bedtime. She may happily jabber to herself for a while in the middle of the night, or cry, but she will soon understand that night time is for sleeping.

Pay close attention to her naps when you are in the new time zone. Don't let her sleep all day (the sleeping baby rule only applies when locked in a vehicle with other passengers). If her normal afternoon nap only lasts for one hour, then do not let her sleep longer, as it will be more difficult for her to adjust to sleeping at night.

In the new time zone, wake the baby in the morning. If she wakes at 5 am at home, do not feel obligated to wake her at 5 am in the new time zone. Rather, wake her at a reasonable morning hour. Always keep the same living patterns, but shift the time accordingly.

Put her to bed in the evening, keeping in mind the customs of the new locale. In Italy, for example, most restaurants don't open for dinner until 8 pm. Parents can be seen strolling with their dolce vita babies at 10 pm. It is fine (and a lot of fun sometimes) to let your baby stay up "late" to keep with your itinerary.

Remember, the schedule is in place so you can easily discern your child's needs. This is particularly important when combating jet lag. Your child may get weary and fussy at times. With a schedule, it is easier to determine whether she is hungry, over-stimulated, hurt, or just plain tired.

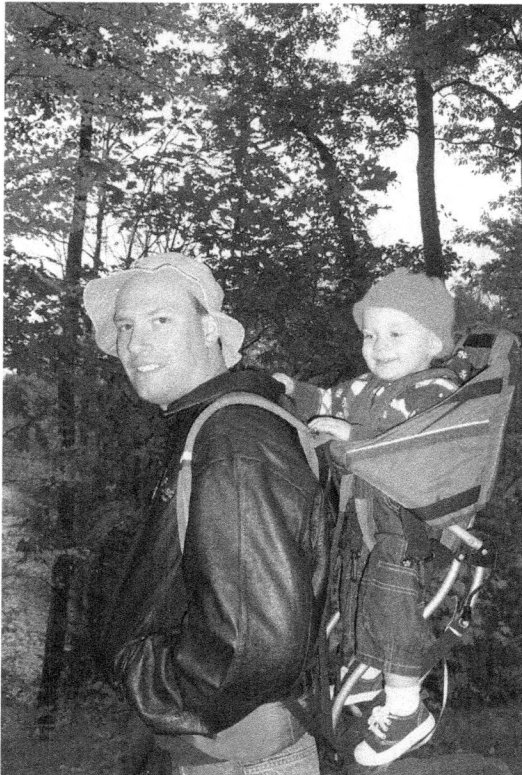

# How to begin introducing flexibility as routine with an infant?

### Feed the baby:

If you are a nursing mother: The easiest way to add flexibility is to eat new foods. Caution: some babies have sensitive stomachs, and foods you consume may cause fussiness in your infant.

Keep track of what you are eating, and give yourself 2 to 3 days before trying another new food. This way, you can know if certain foods are causing any problems for your child.

That said, the wider variety of foods and spices you consume as a mother, the broader the experience for your infant.

If you are giving formula: You may want to try different brands, since the one you favor may not be available on the road. As always, keep careful tabs on how the formula makes baby feel.

With the introduction of solids, you should incorporate a wide range of foods besides peas and carrots. And while jarred foods are most accessible, try making your own. Not only is natural food healthier, the richer flavors expand your baby's palate. A hand babyfood grinder such as the Kid Co Happy Baby is a Gypsy Mama's best friend!

**Take the baby:**

**Many parents are overwhelmed with the thought of taking baby to the neighborhood restaurant, let alone to a different country. Fears of screaming infants keep many poor souls housebound.**

The more you travel with your baby, the easier it will become for both of you. I'm not talking about cross-country train trips either.

Take the baby with you to the store, library, and restaurant. Strap the baby to you, grab a diaper, and out you go.

The sights, sounds, and smells will be imprinted on the child's brain, whether you realize it or not. When the child cries or has a blow-out diaper, you can react calmly, because you're on home turf.

For infants, travel is not something learned in books, it is the motion, the experience that counts. Don't hesitate to take your baby out—it does get easier!

**Talk to baby:**

**Simply looking at your baby and speaking adds to the development of your child's neural pathways.**

Avoid videos, even if they are in a foreign language, as videos can have a negative impact on the neurological function of your child's brain.

However, if you speak more than one language, by all means, use it. It will not confuse your baby or harm her language development. Quite the contrary, speaking a second (or third) language will connect certain neural pathways in your infant's developing brain, which will allow for easy acquisition of language later. If you don't speak a second language? Find out which of your baby's many visitors does. Encourage them to speak to your baby in another language during their visits.

**Talk to strangers:**

**You don't have to dump your baby in the arms of strangers, nor give detailed information on your travel plans. But if travel is your lifestyle, your child will be exposed to many different people across the miles.**

Be protective and wise, but not so defensive and suspicious you cut off the community. Allow your baby to see different faces and hear the nuances of speech of the people around you.

**Routine:**

**If you are in one place for a few weeks, as you may certainly be after you have a baby, establishing a routine can help add flexibility to your child's schedule. Whether you have a general routine or a fixed schedule, you can foresee your child's needs. Don't react to your child's needs; be prepared for them.**

Routines take much of the guesswork out of parenting and allow for an easier adjustment to time-zone crossing. Jet lag is rough, but it is more easily thwarted when you have a routine in which you know what your child needs and when.

If your baby typically eats, has wake time, then naps, (repeat as necessary), you can anticipate what comes next, even if the hours have shifted. You can slowly adjust the routine to fit the new time zone.

Two of my children had strict routines, two did not—so I have seen both sides of the routine issue. Having no routine is akin to fighting wildfires—as soon as you stamp out one problem, another one springs up unexpectedly behind you. It's exhausting to live and to travel that way.

The beauty of an established home routine is that it easily evolves into a flex-routine. That is, a routine which is easily adapted to travel. In the case of my two "easy" travelers, they adjusted their routines themselves by either shifting their wake time or nap time. I was able to keep the pattern the same (sleep, eat, wake), but the hours at which we did those things changed to fit the new time zone.

Practice Makes Perfect!

When your baby is a newborn, traveling is fairly straightforward:

- You do your best to keep baby in his routine
- You flex with the things that are out of your control
- You plan for every possible speed bump you can think of before you leave

Once your baby is a little bigger, and perhaps mobile, things can get a little more "exciting" on the road. Here are a couple of things that we've done over the years to prepare at home, ahead of time, for travel with our little ones.

## Camping In

Our youngest child, Ezra, was by far the most traveled in his first year of life. He was our fourth, so we weren't virgin travel parents when he came along, and we confidently set out on several major journeys.

When he was seven months old (and crawling), we took just the baby and went to Hawaii for two weeks, half business, half pleasure. I spent a lot of time up front thinking about what I would do with this squirmy wormy baby at business dinners that started at bedtime. My solution:

## A Tent

One of those collapsible, pop-up baby tents made for the beach or the backyard turned out to be an absolute godsend. I bought the smallest one he would fit in, set it up in the playpen in the livingroom (where he'd be safe from curious siblings and where the noise level would be higher than in his bedroom), and we practiced napping in it for three weeks before we left.

By the time we hit Hawaii, he was a pro at crashing in his comfy little tent anywhere and everywhere. Our business associates hovered over his little shack in absolute amazement when I'd pop it by the wall behind our table in a swank restaurant and lay him down to rest while I enjoyed my dinner. It also provided sun shade on the beach and a safe place for him to play by the pool while I read my book.

### Piggy Back

Newborns love their carriers. Nine month-olds? Not always! Once your little critter is mobile you may find he's not as excited about being contained in a backpack or sling as he once was.

He wants to get down (on the nasty airport bathroom floor) and explore the world! What's a parent to do? Wrestle him while he screams his head off? If you have to. But it would save everyone's eardrums if your little one learned at home to be content in his carrier.

How do you achieve this? Practice.

Play piggy back. Make it a game. Use the carrier when you don't really need it: in the grocery store, while vacuuming, walking around the block every night. Bounce around, play a game, make it a fun ride for your little tyke, and then when you put him into it for a long day of travel, he's more likely to be excited rather than offended at the containment!

## A Practice Run

A child's first trip usually includes a road trip. If you are driving in your own vehicle, it is very easy to keep the car seat installed. But do you need the stroller, playpen, high chair, "Going to Grandma's" suitcase, baby gym, and toys that won't stop playing music unless you take the batteries out?

If your goal is travel independence, leave the stuff behind.

Use the car seat you have, but bring only a good baby sling or wrap. Sure, having baby in the deluxe carrier/stroller combo might be easy if you're shopping the sales at the mall with Grandma, but if your future includes the cobblestone streets of medieval villages, consider this first road trip easy practice. It will help you get into shape for future trips. Plus, you will have Grandma's arms to rely on, should you need a break.

Make your practice run a purposeful voyage of discovery, experimentation and a time in which to put into action the things you've been working on at home in a brand new setting.

# CHAPTER 8: PACKING & CARRIERS

## What to Bring

In the plethora of information regarding traveling with baby, you will find all sorts of gadgets to "help" you travel. Most of these are completely unnecessary and are cumbersome.

If you want to make travel a part of your lifestyle, and to make it enjoyable, train yourself to do without. Shed the excess baggage while your child is an infant. If simplicity is all the baby knows, she will not demand more as she gets older.

We've discussed the "One Bag Rule" and the principle that less is definitely more when traveling with a baby, but what should go in that shoulder bag you carry onto the airplane, train or overnight ferry?

What does a baby really need for a long day of active travel?

Obviously, the answer to that question will vary somewhat, depending on the age of your infant, and whether or not you have more than one baby. In general, the following pack list should suffice:

- Diapers/Nappies- As many as you would expect to use for one day, plus two more for emergencies

- Bottles-if you are not nursing, bottles and enough formula for one day, plus two feedings for emergencies
- Burp cloth
- One extra outfit for baby
- Wipes- a travel sized package
- One small toy for teething and shaking- preferably one that does not make noise, in consideration of your fellow travelers
- Sling- as a nursing cover up, changing pad, baby carrier, and swaddling blanket
- Your favorite candy bar or comfort food, for when you need a boost

## Carriers Compared

The array of contraptions to move babies from point A to point B is mind boggling.

In this section will compare the most common and make no secret of our personal favourite.

However, it's very important to remember that there's no "right choice," only what works best for you. I have a friend with serious bursitis in her shoulder who cannot bear to wear a sling. I have another friend with an oversized little man who's leg circulation is cut off in a papoose style front carrier. Pick what works best for you and hit the road!

The main consideration is comfort, for Mom and Baby.

## Papoose:

These carriers are the sort that have a pod on the front for baby and padded straps that crisscross behind the parent's back. Baby Bjorn is one of the most popular.

**Pros:** These are often recommended as the best carriers for small babies because they keep the baby close to the parent's body and provide plenty of physical contact for the baby. Some of them convert to carry in other positions and the baby can be carried facing either toward, or away from the parent.

**Cons:** These types of carriers are often very hard on the back. One Mom I know calls them "Mama torture devices." They also have a limited life span as only infants can be carried in them. They tend to be bulky for packing

## Sling:

As you already know, this is our personal favorite!

**Pros:** A sling has multiple uses, folds up into nothing and can double as a diaper bag if it has pockets in the end. It is useful for carrying newborn infants clear through five year-old preschool aged children who have tired feet. It is the most easily washed and dried of the options. I've carried two babies at once in my sling, and it works!

**Cons:** If you have shoulder problems, like bursitis, a sling is NOT for you as it may worsen that condition; try a Maya wrap instead. Some people have trouble getting the hang of how to keep the baby in position in the sling without dropping the child out the bottom. If you're having difficulty with this, practice with a watermelon similar to the size and weight of your baby to be sure you can use it safely.

## Backpack:

Baby backpacks come in a variety of styles. The right choice for your family will depend on your family's type of travel as well as how many kids you hope to use the pack for. In general, we'd recommend spending a little more money and getting one of the expedition grade packs, as they are far better designed ergonomically, and they will last forever: we got five kids out of ours before passing it on in excellent condition to another family!

**Pros**: Most backpacks are designed to grow with your baby; we used ours with kids as old as four. Many have a diaper bag attached as well as a sunshade attached. The ones that are free standing double as a high chair and portable containment for your child when you're on the road, which can be invaluable once they are crawling! Many babies love the motion of riding in a backpack and will nap happily while you walk. The good carriers distribute the weight of the child and pack properly on your hips, so that your back does not get sore. Also, quality carriers can be adjusted according to the frame of the wearer, making it comfortable for Mom or Dad.

**Cons:** You cannot see the baby. If you're traveling alone you'll have to take the pack on and off every time you need to tend to your child. Backpacks should not be used with a child who is not yet sitting up indepencently. They tend to be big and bulky. If you are flying with one, you'll be asked to gate check it like a stroller.

## Carseat:

There are parents who prefer to bring along their child's car seat system to use in planes, trains or taxis as they travel.

**Pros:** Traveling with your child's car seat will ensure maximum safety for your child in all situations on airplanes, trains or in taxi cabs. You will be sure it is fitted properly to your child and is clean. It will provide a safe, comfortable spot to put your baby down that smells like home and feels "normal" to your baby.

**Cons:** Car seats are a lot of work to lug through airports and train stations, especially if you are traveling alone with your baby. They can be rented by almost all car rental agencies upon arrival. Car seat regulations vary greatly by state, province and country. It is important, if you choose to take your own, that you make sure that it meets the requirements of your destination.

# CHAPTER 9: HELP! I'VE GOT A SCREAMER!

## We're trapped on the plane! Why is the baby crying?

Infants' needs are fairly basic. A crying baby on a plane (or in a car, or anywhere else) usually means one of the following is wrong:

**A medical problem:**

On airplanes, this is likely due to ear pressure. During takeoff and landing, you may be asked to hold your child up to your shoulder. If this is the case, the old advice on feeding your infant during takeoff and landing may not be possible.

If your infant takes a pacifier, try to use it to alleviate ear pressure. If your baby prefers a thumb or fingers, help her to do so if cabin pressure is a problem. If your baby is old enough, try placing an all-natural, easily-dissolved teething tablet on her tongue. The sucking motion will provide relief as cabin pressure changes.

On a road trip, if your baby has spent hours in a carseat and has been unable to wiggle about as he's used to, it's very possible that he's suffering with intestinal gas. There are several things you can do to help a child in this predicament.

- Be proactive, be careful to avoid gas inducing foods and burp the baby thoroughly after every feeding.
- Stop the car BEFORE there's screaming and get the baby out of the carseat and moving every hour or so for a few minutes.
- Play "bicycle" with his legs and help get those bubbles moving through.
- Carry gas drops or gripe water in your medical kit to help relieve the pain once it's started.

## Discomfort:

Those jeans from BabyGap are cute, but the elastic may be digging into your child's midsection. Dress baby in a one-piece outfit that can be layered. Also, pants with thick elastic can push down the diaper, leaving you vulnerable to the dreaded diaper blowout.

## Hunger:

If you have a routine established, you should know when your child is hungry, and when she simply wants comfort. Feed the baby according to her normal schedule and avoid comfort feeding.

Comfort feeding can lead to a less satisfying meal, more frequent 'snacking,' and even stomach upset. Try to comfort her in other ways. Yes, the passengers around you may scowl, but that's when you smile, apologize, and pass out the ear plugs.

## Diaper:

What goes in must come out again. If you've been feeding the baby more frequently than normal, you will go through more diapers. This is where a schedule can be invaluable. If you know your baby's needs, you will not have to worry about the extra diapers.

On a plane, try to have the baby in a dry diaper before takeoff because it may be a while before you are allowed to move about the cabin. The illuminated seatbelt sign shows no mercy.

## Sleepy:

If your child likes to stretch out when sleeping, you may opt for the bassinet on the airline. If this option is for you, make sure to contact the airline to reserve the bassinet.

One caution: if your baby is a good traveler and a good sleeper, being in the row next to other crying babies may not be ideal for you. If your baby is a cuddler, the sling or wrap is the best place.

If you're on a road trip, try to plan your drive times around when your baby is most likely to be asleep anyway. This will reduce stress on the baby, and on the grown-ups!

## Overstimulation:

Sometimes the sights are just too much for baby. If she has a light blanket, try creating some privacy by draping it loosely over her and talking to her gently. A sling or wrap can also give needed privacy and keep the baby from being upset by too much action.

## For no reason whatsoever:

Babies cry: it's a fact of life. There are times when you can't quite figure it out. Keep in mind, you are helping your baby learn to travel, and quite often, there are tears involved. And once baby finds her voice, you may be in for some decibels that make canines tip their heads. Stay calm, don't worry, and above all, do not laugh when she screams.

The more adept you are at anticipating and correctly discerning your baby's needs, the easier travel becomes for the entire family.

## We're trapped on the plane! And my baby is screaming for fun!

"Mama," "Dada," "bow-wow," "want 'dat," as your baby learns to assemble sounds into words, he is also discovering volume control. Babies develop skills through repetition. So certain behaviors, whether for good or for ill, will be constantly repeated, and repeated, and repeated…

In addition to acquiring new skills through repetition, your baby is learning to use behavior to elicit parental reaction. When he says, "mama" you gush. But what to do when he screams?

At this stage of life, babies will not do something "bad" out of disobedience, they have no concept of "bad," or "good," for that matter. Your child is simply using a newly acquired skill in order to get a reaction from you.

This is one of those times in your child's life when you will need more balance than a tight-rope walker. You cannot ignore the behavior, yet you should never punish a baby for a natural behavior.

Here's how I've dealt with screamers (and yes, I did have a couple of them):

### Ho-hum. Did you say something?

When your baby screams for fun, above all, remain calm. Even if your ears are bursting and your eyes are watering, try to act unfazed. The bigger reaction baby gets from you, the more he will repeat the behavior.

### Talk like Tofu:

Soft and firm: those words should describe your tone of voice when reacting to screaming.

Speaking softly, yet firmly in baby's ear will often make him pause in order to listen. Tell the baby "quiet" (or whichever word you prefer). I try to avoid the word "no" because there will be times when you can let your child scream for fun (think, on the playground). Your child may only be a baby, but it is possible to train him the proper time and place for quiet.

## Close the loopholes:

Don't let the behavior s ide—not even once. For if baby discovers a loophole, it will be exploited; and then you'll be starting all over again. As with most things regarding the travel training of babies, there is no quick fix. Be consistent and steadfast, even if you begin to feel like an elementary school librarian.

Deal with the screaming issue now, and do not put it off until the child is three (when he adds artistry, such as flailing).

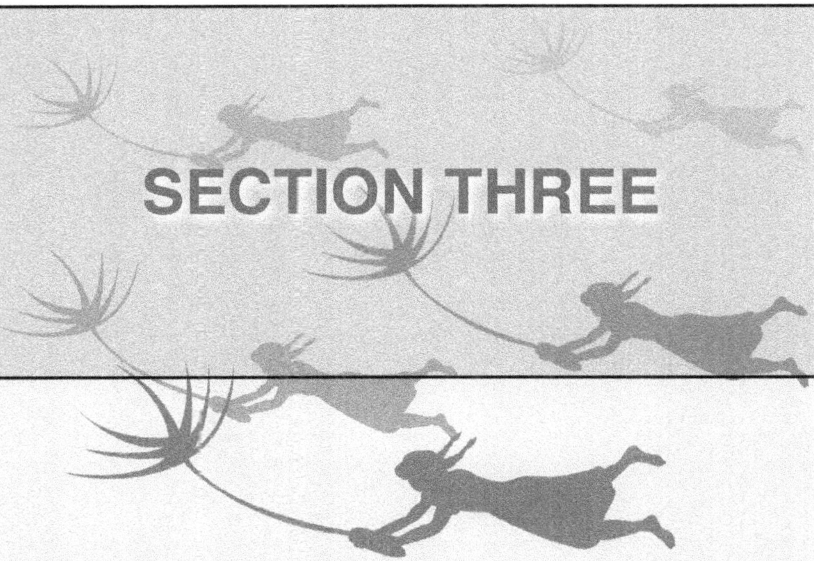

## SECTION THREE

# TRAVEL WITH TODDLERS

# CHAPTER 10: INTRO TO TODDLER TRAVEL

Congratulations! You are about to enter the most intense travel-training time of your child's life.

Potty training, temper tantrums, the dreaded willful disobedience, and a host of issues you've never imagined will rear their heads during this time. It is the toddler years in which your child will fearlessly assert independence, while learning to push your buttons.

Before you conceal the passports in your sock drawer, let me add that the toddler years provide some of the most hilarious, most charming and intimate moments of your traveling life.

The toddler years are not the time to give up travel. They are the most crucial when it comes to training. By being consistent, fair, and persistent, you will emerge these years with more travel freedom than you ever thought possible.

Believe it or not, by the time your child is 30 months old, he can learn to:

- Sit in an airline seat secured only by the lap belt (without kicking the seat in front of him)
- Carry his own backpack
- Walk next to you without a humiliating "baby leash"
- Ride in a sling or backpack without a fuss
- NOT touch artifacts or works of art worth more than the GNP of small countries
- Heed the words stop, quiet, and no

These goals are possible, and we know because we've been there!

Between the two of us, we've survived toddlerhood nine times!

We've managed toddlers with bigger kids, toddlers with infants and even weathered four under four years old, still managing international travel. These may seem like Herculean feats, but they are nothing compared to what you will go through.

Take heart: travel with toddlers will, truly, be some of the best times in your life.

I will never forget soaking in a hot tub under the immense night sky of the Sonora Desert, my toddler pointing up excitedly at the moon (he was born in Alaska—it was too cold for stargazing with toddlers). Or discovering a trail of leaf cutter ants with a delighted three year-old whilst hiking the jungle trails around Coba, in Mexico. There are a million toddler-travel stories that form the basis of our family's lore.

I wouldn't trade one of those stories, not even the bad ones, for anything in the world.

These experiences have knit us together as a family. The results are not always beautiful, (you'll read about our Fresh Fruit Folly and the Green Mountain Boy later), but every flaw taught us something new.

## Why Travel With Toddlers?

If your toddler invents new ways of getting into trouble in a controlled environment (such as his own room), why would you bring him into the wide world? Wouldn't it be better to postpone travel until he has more self-control?

Take a good look at that little person strewing toys across the living room:

From the time he was born until now, his cerebral cortex has developed over a hundred trillion synapses. Synapses may seem of little concern to you, as your toddler flings his oatmeal at the wall. But synapses are the link between neurons which form the basis for emotion, relationships, language, and motor skills. At this point in your child's life, he has an overabundance of these synapses. As he repeats a behavior, he is strengthening particular neural pathways. These sensory experiences stimulate chemical reactions on the microscopic level, which literally shapes not only what he knows, but how he utilizes it.

117

The good news is that by repeating a particular behavior, you can help your child learn to be an excellent young nomad. The bad news? It requires patience—loads of it.

Toddlerhood is not the time to stop travel training. Neural pathways in your child's brain that are not strengthened through repetition of experience will be pruned, or cut off. It is the brain's way of deciding what information is useful and what is not. If your toddler is repeatedly exposed to travel scenarios or savvy traveler habits, his brain will establish neural pathways that endure, thus shaping him to be a great little adventurer.

Remember the last time you used new software (without doing the tutorial first)? It may have been frustrating: the icons were unfamiliar or in strange places, the wording was different, and you felt like you couldn't find your way around. But the more you used the program, the more skill you developed. It was only through exposure and repetition you became adept at navigating the new program.

Similarly, a child's brain is programmed through exposure and repetition. The brain is taking in sensory information and organizing it. Your child's reaction to stimuli will be shaped by prior experience. By exposing him to travel scenarios at a young age, or by repeating good travel behaviors, you are equipping your child for the travel lifestyle.

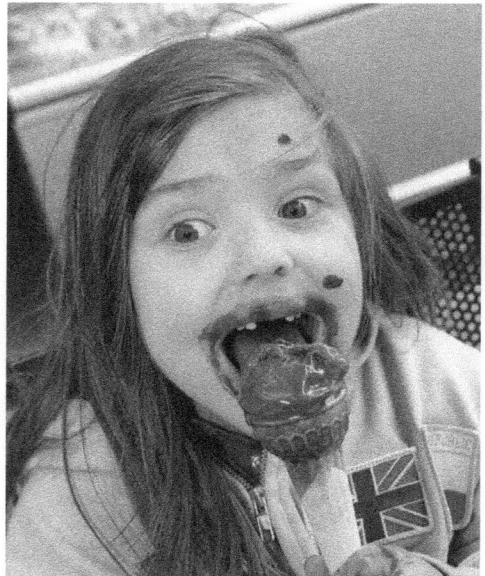

118

# CHAPTER 11: TRAVEL TRAIN YOUR TODDLER

## Behavior: What We're All Afraid Of!

At first blush, toddlers don't appear to be very travel friendly creatures. They are often loud, messy, and are prone to precipitous mood swings resulting in either hyper-happy running, or uber-angry meltdowns. These extremes lead many parents to baton down the hatches, stay home for a few years and weather the storm.

What many parents overlook is that toddlers are eager learners and willing participants in most any game, which we big people can use to our infinite advantage in training these little creatures to LOVE travel.

Yes, toddlerhood can be (will be) rocky at times. Yes, there will be temper f ts and meltdowns and moments of hyper mania. But there will also be times of unbelievable sweetness and more moments pregnant with educational possibility than can possibly be counted.

For a family with wanderlust, there is no reason not to turn these tumultuous toddler years into some of the best travel experiences of a lifetime. While it's true that your child may not carry long term memories of his L'Ouvre visit at three into adulthood, the experiences he has as a little elf will certainly shape who he becomes over the years. We are all the cumulative result of our life experience, why not expose your toddler to a few things bigger than Sesame Street and a few characters grander than Elmo? In this section we'll discuss concrete ways you can train your toddler to be ready to tackle the world.

To Teach Travel Safe Skills: Play Games!

Travel-training a toddler often includes blood, sweat, and tears (so don't forget the bandages and tissues). Don't be intimidated: toddlers can be successfully trained for travel.

Raise your standards above what society expects, yet never expect perfection.

Whether you have decided to take a break from the nomadic life, or not, there are many ways to prepare your child around your home base for future adventures.

Pull out a travel guide from your shelf. Take a look at the section that says, "Traveling with Children." It might be hard to find: a paragraph or two at the end of the book. If you're lucky it's an entire page. I don't know what city or country you're perusing, but I will wager this part of the book has one or more of the following listed:

- A zoo
- A park
- A park where people walk around dressed as cartoon characters
- A "hands-on" museum (or pseudo-science museum, as I like to call them)
- A theater that offers a 3D movie
- A museum with mechanical dinosaurs

If these are your only options for sight-seeing with Junior, no wonder you'd rather stay home. There is a time and a place for everything; and a park is a great place for kids to let off steam, but with a little creativity, so is any open grassy area. And unless the zoo or park is particularly spectacular or unique to the region you're in (say, a safari in Africa), it is a waste of precious time to go there.

Don't child-proof your travel; travel-proof your child.

With a little imagination, you can train your child to explore the Musée d'Orsay without grabbing the Monets. But it doesn't happen overnight: it begins at home.

# First steps

As a parent, my primary concern is to keep my child safe while traveling. Toddlers are particularly notorious for getting into all sorts of trouble. Travel-training a toddler is as challenging and exhilarating as an Everest ascent. As in every journey, it begins with a first few steps.

It amuses me (especially after we are through airport security) to see a toddler sporting a harness. Usually it is spruced up with a cuddly bear to help you forget you have now leashed your child like a wayward puppy. From the time your baby graduates to toddler, he can be trained to follow or walk beside you.

Now, there are definitely times when you should not train your toddler. And obviously, you don't want to throw your little one into a crowded metro station and expect him to hop on the right tube. But you can begin at home by playing a few games that will teach your child to follow you.

Here's how it works:

First, Choose A Safety Zone. Begin in a place where Junior can move about without majorly disturbing anyone, and where he cannot escape. This could be your living room or a fenced-in yard or park. Make sure it is a place with few, less-alluring distractions. An indoor play center might be safe, but your toddler (to your dismay) will choose the ball pit over Mama any day of the week. Initial training should also be in a place where it will not inconvenience others, and where your child will be absolutely safe. Don't worry! You will be able to hop on a tuk-tuk someday—it's just not a good place to begin.

# Introducing... The Games!

### Come to Mama (or Papa)

The purpose of the game: To create a happy, safe space and to make your arms the place your child delights in.

### Follow The Leader

The purpose of the game: To create happy ducklings who are impervious to distractions!

### Halt!

The purpose of the game: To make it FUN to stop on a dime.

### Chasing Fun

The purpose of the game: Role reversal to reinforce the FUN of following.

Come to Mama (or Papa). This is a game that comes naturally as a parent. From the moment your baby launches himself from the coffee table to the sofa, you coax him towards you. Even when he has found his toddler legs and is off and running, continue this game.

Begin by sitting on the floor. Whenever he comes to you, it should be as if he's won a prize. When you are in your safety zone, get up and move around a bit. His arrival should signal a celebration: scoop him up for a kiss, hold him upside-down, or give a high-five. Whichever method you choose, make it a mini-party.

Follow-the-leader. It's an old game with a practical purpose —training your child to follow you. People used to laugh at the sight of me with four kids following like ducklings. But it is much easier to lead ducklings than to herd geese.

Following begins as a game in the toddler years. It is enjoyable but extremely practical. So march around your safety zone and encourage your toddler to follow you. It's a great way for you to spend time with your toddler while developing an important travel skill. As your child becomes better at following, you can slowly add distractions.

Halt! Teaching your child to freeze in place is just as important as teaching him to follow. No matter how adept your toddler is at following you, he will break away eventually.

When playing follow-the-leader, we incorporated the word "halt." You can say "stop" or "freeze" if you like. The point is the same. Whenever we halted in our march, the kids would freeze (usually while making funny gestures). I would let them run ahead of me in certain areas then call "halt." If one of them moved even a toe, he or she would lose. Halting was fun—a part of the game rather than an arbitrary command.

Halting is one of the most critical traveling skills your child can possess. Obviously, it is useful with toddlers because they are unable to see danger. But halting is also useful in later years. My eldest (who was ten at the time) would have been hit by a car in Prague if not for his quick reaction to the word "halt."

Chasing fun. If you wish to travel-train your toddler, the last thing you should do is encourage a game where escape is the goal.

Sure, it is great fun to pretend you're a monster and run through the house after your giggling toddler. But it's an entirely different ballgame when your son instigates a game of chase while you're waiting for the ICE train to Amsterdam.

> Though you are giving commands, you do not have to raise your voice. Your child should be attuned to your normal speaking voice. If he cannot hear your command, he is too far away. For the sake of other travelers, a parent should not sound like a drill sergeant. The only exception is when there is a critical situation, such as a car running a red light as your child steps off the curb. In that case, the word automatically explodes into the stratosphere.

If you want to play chase with your toddler, reverse the roles. Encourage your child to chase you. This helps to develop the "following" skill, and allows for a lot of fun. Training is serious business, but it should not be joyless.

## Independence Day

**Your toddler has probably already discovered a myriad of ways of asserting autonomy. Rather than banning independence, administer it in appropriate doses.**

When your toddler is able to halt nine times out of ten during follow-the-leader, expand his horizons.

Move from the safety zone to a location where there are a few more distractions.

- Graduate him to new places as his travel skills develop.
- Take him to the local hands-on museum (where they encourage kids to grab stuff).
- Allow him some discovery time, but also do your follow-the-leader routine.
- See what happens when you say, "Halt."

Good results? Then you're ready for the big time! Take him to the grocery store. Don't buckle him into the metal jail on wheels, but let him walk. The worst that can happen is he pulls a few canned goods off the shelf, or he knocks over an end display. Humiliating, maybe; dangerous, not really.

The perfect place to allow for a bit of toddler independence is in the airport. Read that again: it was not a misprint.

If you are not bogged down by excess baggage, you will be entirely capable of travel-training a toddler in the airport. Here are a few guidelines:

- Go through security first
- Move far away from the exit
- Begin after you bypass the entrance for the moving walkway
- Hold his hand if you want (or if he allows)
- Play "Halt!" to test the waters

- Be his "eyes on the road," as toddlers see everything except the danger directly in front of them

Obviously, going through security means you are in an area with other ticketed passengers. You are not as exposed to thieves and kidnappers in this area. Though you should always remain alert, this secured area is a good place to begin allowing toddler-sized independence.

An additional benefit of travel-training in the airport is you have quick access to security personnel, should an emergency arise.

# Why unleash the toddler?

As a parent, it can be a fearful thing to allow your child out of your hands in a crowd. But "out of your hands" is not synonymous with "out of control." Allowing your toddler small, frequent portions of autonomy will satisfy his craving, rather than leaving him hungry for more.

Not only are you giving your child a bit of the independence he desires, but you are creating a solid base of experience upon which all future travel is built. A four year-old who has been strapped into a stroller his entire life is simply not equipped for a 4 year-old level of independence. The unequipped child can be an annoyance to other people, as well as a danger to himself.

If you establish good travel habits through training and allow bits of independence in age-appropriate ways, your child is less likely to rebel against what he considers arbitrary rules.

# CHAPTER 12: MANAGING BEHAVIOR

## Managing Behavioral Issues

While each child has a distinct way of interacting with the world, several themes tend to crop up when talking about toddlers. There may seem to be no rhyme or reason to it. One of your children may appear independent enough to have her own apartment already, while the other frequently re-ties herself to your apron strings.

Personality and temperament cannot always be explained. Behavioral issues seem amplified while on the road because you do not want to impose upon your fellow travelers. If you are entertaining the idea of travel-training your toddler, you may be concerned about one or more of the following typical behaviors:

### Aggression

Kicking, hitting, hair-pulling or biting: aggressive behavior puts a damper on the travel dreams of many parents. There are two main reasons for aggressive outbursts: simple anger and attention-seeking.

### Anger

Anger is a natural feeling in human beings. The goal is not to avoid anger or to bury it, but rather to express it in healthy ways. How does a toddler express anger? During

131

that fine timeline between babyhood and toddlerhood, children may act out aggressively. If a toy is taken away, the toddler does not have the verbal skills to talk about his problem. So, he hits or bites. This is not the kind of social interaction you want to bring with you to foreign countries.

## Prevention

With toddlers, it is always best if you can prevent an outburst. If you see your child simmering, try to fix the situation before he heats up to a rolling boil. If you know a special toy will cause a conflict, remove it before the play date.

It is not that you can insulate your child from every troublesome situation, and certainly, travel will bring many challenges, but you should never deliberately set up your toddler for failure.

By age 2 ½ to 3, these social concepts, such as sharing, or talking about anger develop more fully.

## Consequences

If your child lashes out in anger, what should you do?

All instructions given to your toddler should be given in your Tofu Voice: soft, yet firm.

Gently correct the anger outburst. Then, determine the most appropriate consequences for the action. If he is in conflict with another child over a particular toy, then the toy should go away. "Then they'll both be crying," you say. The point is not to prevent tears (as if that were humanly possible), but to assert logical consequences for a particular action. The removing of toys, objects, or privileges is a great way for a toddler to link bad behavior with loss—something he will wish to avoid.

It is important to be lovingly firm, and consistent.

### Attention-seeking

The second reason for aggressive behavior is that the child is simply looking for a reaction in the parent.

Usually, the reason bad behavior is reinforced is due to overreaction in the parent. The child learns quickly which behavior elicits the biggest and quickest parental response. If your toddler yanks a handful of your hair, he may laugh while you cry. It's not that you're raising a young Machiavelli; the toddler is simply learning to get a reaction from you. It is a matter of cause and effect.

### Consequences

Above all, do not overreact.

Behaviors that send you into overdrive when your child is two, will make you chuckle with amusement when you've weathered the storm and see some other child doing the same thing.

Certainly you must deal with the behavior, but remember that parenthood is a marathon not a sprint. Decide what words you want to use: "be gentle," "that hurts mommy," or whatever phrase you prefer. Talk to him in your calm, firm voice while unwinding your hair from his chubby little fingers. Take away the temptation by putting him down for a minute. Then give him another chance.

As long as you are consistent, your toddler will learn the rules eventually.

### Excessive Crying

Unless your child has a serious medical problem, excessive crying is usually a mere performance.

For an infant, crying is a vital part of communication. By the toddler years, the child is capable of developing alternate methods of communication, such as pointing, using sign language, or by saying simple words.

You cannot get through this stage of life without a few toddler tears. It's impossible. But you can prevent excessive crying. It is vital to take on this challenge now, rather than in a few years.

## Prevention

Don't swoop up your child and lavish him with kisses every time he whimpers.

As long as you are observing the situation, there is no harm in letting him cry a little. Give him a chance to settle the situation himself before you come rushing in.

### Whining

Whining is very similar to crying. It is a tool in your toddler's belt, used to manipulate a situation. From the time our children were waddling around, whining was not an option. Whining was immediately corrected—especially when the sacred name of "Mama" was conveyed in a whiney manner.

Whining comes naturally to little ones, but if it sticks, it is because the child has learned that this voice tone is rewarded.

## Response

Whining should get no response other than a firm, calm word or phrase, delivered in your tofu voice.

Since we tried to avoid overusing the word "no," whining was countered with the phrase, "talk with words." If your toddler isn't talking yet, assess the situation and give him the phrase he is looking for. Watch for his non-verbal cues to see if you were right.

Or to avoid whining in your non-verbal toddler, teach a few hand signs. It will alleviate frustration on both parts, and it will not interfere with your child's acquisition of language.

Teach your child to use appropriate voice tone in her efforts to communicate!

Have you ever been seated on an airplane in front of someone's whiny child? Or at a restaurant next to the child who gets everything by whining? Please, for the sake of your fellow man, and to create a shining example of good ambassadorship, ditch this behavior while your kid is young!

## Shyness

There is nothing wrong with a child being a little shy. And most toddlers will have a leeriness of strangers, which is completely natural. But if your child screams when she loses sight of you, your life will quickly become exhausting.

You may think the shy child is the best traveler, after all, when traveling, she won't be out of your sight. However, the clingy child will cry when she loses sight of you, not when you lose sight of her. I had a clingy child who would cry when she couldn't see me—even if we were in the same car (and she could see the back of my head).

## The Solution

Some children are naturally more reserved than others. But extreme shyness can be overcome through training.

Ease your child into new situations.

- Introduce her to new people from the safety of your lap.
- Don't let her bury herself in your arms, but teach her how to shake hands.
- Begin at home by pretending to visit other people— use their names and teach her to shake hands or give high-fives to her stuffed animals.
- Then try it with people you know.

- When she interacts with people while sitting with you, try having her sit next to you.

Since toddlers more easily identify behavior with objects, use a small blanket (a flannel baby blanket works well) at home while you read. Have her sit on the blanket (repeatedly) while you read. After several sessions, she will understand that the blanket is her sitting place. Once she is comfortable with the blanket, take her to story time at the public library.

Sit next to her, with her blanket spread out in the group. If she only wants to be held, remove her from the group, and sit next to her on the periphery. You want to slowly broaden her horizons without pushing too quickly.

*Caution: you will be tempted by the presence of other people to give in to your child's crying or whining—don't do it. As long as you aren't stretching your child too quickly, stick with the plan.

### Food Throwing

I have never met a toddler who did not throw food at some point.

### Avoiding It

Again, using your tofu voice, discourage the behavior. Also, make sure your toddler isn't snacking too much between meal times. Whether your toddler eats several smaller meals a day or three bigger meals a day, make sure extra snacks (including milk or juice) aren't filling him up between meals.

Another tactic is to not place the entire meal in front of your little pitcher, rather, give him only a little bit of food at a time. This way he can take the appropriate portion, and there is less to clean up, should he toss it on the floor.

If he is simply throwing and not eating, he may not be hungry. Take him out of the situation and wait until he is actually hungry. If you are in a restaurant? Take the food away, and offer bite sized portions. Also, encourage interest in the eating process by giving him a toddler-safe spoon or fork.

Still tossing his food? Remove the plate altogether.

Remember, keep calm and show minimal reaction while enforcing consequences.

## Screaming

As babies develop into toddlers, they experiment with a variety of behaviors. Screaming is one of these. If you began discouraging screaming while your child was an infant, then he should be through the screaming-for-fun stage. By toddlerhood, your child will yell or scream in an effort to gain attention.

## Response

Ho-hum. Did you say something? When your toddler screams for fun, it is imperative to remain calm. Even if your ears are bursting and your eyes are watering, try to act unfazed. Remember, the bigger your reaction, the more you reinforce your toddler's behavior (even if it's bad).

Talk like Tofu Soft and firm: those words should describe your tone of voice when reacting to screaming. Get down at your toddler's level, look him in the eyes, and speak softly and firmly. Tell him "quiet," or "talk softly," or whatever phrase suits you best.

Your child may only be a toddler, but he is entirely capable of learning times and places for being quiet. As a junior world traveler, knowing when to be quiet is extremely important.

Close the loopholes Don't let the behavior slide—not even once. If your toddler discovers a loophole, it is bound to be exploited; and then you'll be starting all over again. As with most things regarding the travel training of toddlers, there is no quick fix.

## Getting into things

In her quest to explore this new world, your toddler will get into things.

She will open doors, drawers, cupboards.

- She will place things inside boxes, including herself.
- She will discover things around the house you didn't know existed.

While you want to encourage exploration of your little adventurer, you have to set boundaries. You may travel to places that are not toddler-proofed, and your child's safety will depend upon prior training.

## Solution

It comes back to doling out toddler-sized portions of independence.

If your toddler is courageous enough to explore places, then teach her how to do it in the appropriate manner. If she is opening doors at home, let her try it when you are out and about. Even if you have to help her in her struggle, she will feel like she is accomplishing something great. Take her shopping, and allow her to hand you items to put into the basket. Teach her the words "slowly" or "gently."

If you are flying, bring a small gift box—the thin kind used for sweaters or coffee mugs work great. It packs flat, requires no tape for assembly, and can be thrown away at the end of the trip. For the toddler who enjoys getting into things, a simple box can keep her busy for hours. If you can't find a gift box, a brown paper lunch bag is another way to keep her interest, though these can be loud in confined places.

Allow your child to open doors (or to try), climb stairs, push the appropriate elevator button, carry her own backpack, or give the airline ticket to the flight attendant. These activities are appropriate ways to allow your child to explore her world.

If you grant her some independence now, she is more likely to obey you when you tell her "stop" or "don't touch."

Whatever behavioral issue you face, it can be tempered with a calm yet firm response. Stay consistent and do not change the rules in an effort to keep your young traveler quiet.

You will endure tears and tantrums while your child is a toddler, and as a traveler, these things are downright embarrassing. But if you do not expose her to travel situations, there is no way she can learn. It is far more disturbing to deal with outbursts from school aged children than it is from toddlers.

Toddlerhood is the time for training. It is when your child is the most pliable (no matter how stubborn he seems). Do everything you can to help shape those neural pathways towards building solid travel savvy behaviors.

# Rules, Consequences, and the Reason Why

For their own safety, children who travel must have set rules. But rules without consequences are empty and unlikely to be heeded.

Before your child reaches toddler age, think about consequences for certain behaviors. Don't let situations take you by surprise. If you are unequipped to handle a behavioral issue, you are more likely to be led by emotion, which can be detrimental to your relationship with your child and to the travel training process.

When a parent is unprepared for a situation, she is most likely to either revert to how she was raised, or the opposite of how she was raised. It is much healthier if you, as a parent, think through scenarios and how you will handle them.

Take what was good from your upbringing and use it, leave what was bad. You and your spouse are creating new rules for new kids. It is up to you to decide how to handle certain situations. But it isn't easy to do this on the fly.

Think about rules and meaningful consequences before you are faced with a toddler meltdown during that 4 hour layover in Chicago.

I have a rebellious streak. It is a personal flaw that often gets me into trouble. If someone tells me I must do something a particular way, my first instinct is to do the opposite. However, if I am told the reason something must be done in a particular way, I am absolutely willing to go along.

Rules often appear arbitrary unless they are backed up with a "reason why."

You may have a child who is like this: one who seems to learn everything the hard way. One key to helping this child is to simply tell him the reason why.

If you give him a rule, such as "don't touch," make sure you add "because the cactus will sting your finger." Even if you think your toddler is incapable of understanding, he may comprehend more than you realize. Furthermore, it develops a routine for you as a parent—a habit you fall into, which will prevent, in many cases, willful disobedience.

As you travel, you may find yourself questioning the rules of behavior you have established. Why should the child refrain from kicking the airline seat in front of him? Why should he not scream at people for fun? Because it is annoying, is the obvious answer. But the real answer lies deeper.

One concept we have tried to instill in our children is ambassadorship.

As ambassadors, it is the duty of our entire family to promote understanding and to develop good relationships with real-life people around the globe.

The reason why toddlers should not scream or kick is not simply because it's annoying but because all people are precious.

Misbehavior affects the people around you (disturbs the peace, as I tell the kids).

Rules of behavior during travel are not arbitrary—almost everything boils down to preserving the idea that all people are important.

**Don't cave in!**

The toddler years could be called the "no" years. You may find yourself saying this repeatedly. Trust me, it will end, eventually. But it is imperative that "no" from a parent means "no;" not "ask a hundred times then I'll say yes."

**It is important for the building of trust that you stick to your word and be consistent.** No amount of crying because your little tyke is unhappy with a parental decree should move you.

# CHAPTER 13: PICKY EATERS & TRAVEL

We've all met a child who turns his nose up at everything but chicken nuggets.

As new parents we FEAR the food battles to come. Why is it that one child will happily trade macaroni and cheese for couscous, and peanut butter with jelly sandwiches for flat bread with roasted garlic and kalmata olives without batting an eyelash, and another child insist on carrot sticks with ranch dip and a side of sliced apples for every meal on every continent? If there were one answer to that question, someone would be making millions!

The truth is that some kids are just picky eaters, while others aren't.

All kids go through phases of preferring some foods over others, and a wise parent learns to roll with the punches, not make a mountain out of a mole hill, and works patiently with her child's nutritional quirks.

Sometimes, what appears to be picky eating (eating only a tiny bit of what is served) is actually just the child's tiny stomach filling quickly. The American Academy of Pediatrics defines a child's serving size as one measuring tablespoon of food for each year of age. That means a two year-old will only need two tiny tablespoons of mashed potatoes. Get out your baking spoons and look at how little that really is!

143

While some kids just don't eat much, others are truly picky. If you're saddled with one of the latter, there are a few things you can try to diversify your child's nutritional portfolio.

- Don't introduce processed foods. These tend to be full of empty calories and artificial additives that make them more palatable to little people and can cause them to prefer foods that are less nutritionally dense.
- Fix one meal. If one meal is fixed for the family and the child is welcome to eat it, or not, he will eventually join the family in eating.
- Rule out allergies. Sometimes a child's aversion to certain foods is his body's way of protecting itself.
- Cover the food groups in the course of a day. Don't allow your child to fixate on just fruits, or only orange vegetables. Provide a variety of food groups during meal and snack time.
- Introduce the "No, thank you" bite. Before you allow a child to turn up his nose, insist she take one bite before saying, "No, thank you." This simple practice will save embarrassment and hurt feelings when you find yourself in a culture in which refusing to eat what you're served is the height of rudeness.
- Let him help cook. Sometimes something as simple as letting a child help prepare a new food will encourage him to taste it too!

## Dealing With Pickiness

Dealing with mealtime pickiness can be trying at home. It is often even more difficult whilst traveling. Having to hunt far and wide for *something* your child might eat and then hope it meets with his approval is stressful! Here are a few tips that may help:

- Look for foods that fall into the general categories your child enjoys: fruits, cheeses, or crackers, for example.
- Pack food along. If you can, bring a stash of the foods your child loves the most for just such difficult moments. Sometime structuring for success is the best option!
- Relax. Visible stress on the part of the parent only escalates the child's anxiety as well. Even if Junior refuses a couple of meals in a row, he is NOT going to starve himself to death before you find something he's willing to eat. It will be okay!

## Food As Comfort

We all know that sometimes food provides comfort. Hot tea soothes my nerves at the end of a long day. A scoop of ice cream relaxes my husband before bed. Children take comfort in certain foods too.

If a particular food is part of your child's daily comfort routine, like a glass of warm milk before bed, be sure to include that when you're traveling as well.

When we set off for a year's cycle through Europe and North Africa our kids made a lot of adjustments, not the least of which were nutritional. They gave up many of their favorite American comfort foods and in turn fell in love with a few new international ones. It was, perhaps, hardest on our youngest who dejectedly observed that real Italian pizza was a poor approximation of his US favorite and kippers made a poor breakfast substitute for bacon.

One morning, on the edge of the Sahara desert, I asked, "What would you children like to have for lunch?" Ezra looked wistfully into the distance and replied, "I'd really love a peanut butter sandwich, but I suppose we'll just have couscous...."

It was the request I'd been waiting eight months for: peanut butter. Hidden in the bottom of my bicycle pannier was a lonely little jar of peanut butter just waiting to be missed badly enough by some woebegone American child--today, was its day.

That jar of nut butter elicited whooping and hopping around like grasshoppers on speed on the part of my children. Those lunch sandwiches were eaten with the ceremony usually reserved for four course meals in five star restaurants.

The moral of the story: no matter where you're going, or how long you'll be gone, pack comfort food--you'll eventually need it.

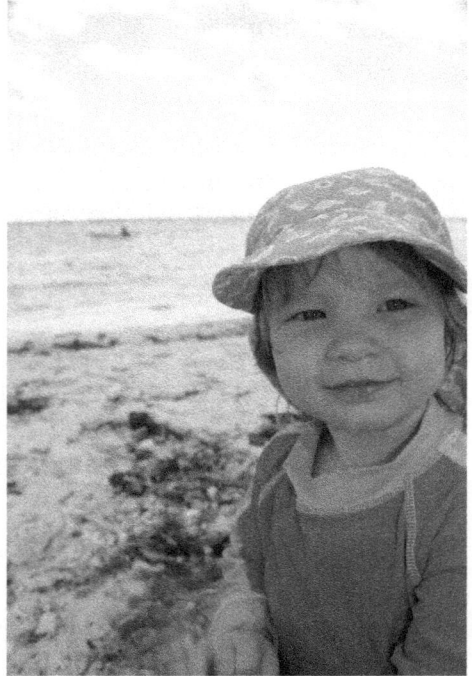

# CHAPTER 14: POTTY TRAINING & TRAVEL

Every parent, psychologist, pediatrician, in-law, and stranger on the bus has an opinion on toilet training. You will be vehemently assured this-or-that method works best.

I am not here to proclaim what will work best for your child's temperament and disposition (my own children were vastly different from one another). I am here to tell you what has worked for our family and to encourage you it is possible to potty train while on the road.

If your child is ready, then do not hesitate to begin. It is hard work, but once done successfully, it leads to much more travel freedom.

## The One Week Method

The most effective way we found to potty train was to set aside one week for the task.

We found a location that was ideal: a hot climate and an apartment with stone floors. The warm climate is good because in the one-week method, your child will be wearing a long shirt or dress, and that's about it. Hard floors are best simply because they are easy to clean up. And if the floors are easy to clean up, you will be more relaxed about the whole process .

Some people choose to let the child go without underpants. But as I was training a budding fashionista, a pack of pretty underwear to keep from getting soiled turned out to be a good motivator.

It was very simple, for one week, my child went around in big girl underpants. If she made a mess on the floor, she helped clean it up. I did not have to stress or hover around her.

Yes, she made messes the first day. When she made a mess, we would dump out her underpants in the toilet if we had to, and she would don the rubber gloves and help clean up. By the second day, she was running to the potty in anticipation, rather than after the fact.

After the first week, she had learned to read the signals of her own body. While she sometimes had to be reminded to use the potty, after week one I could take her to the store, the market, or a restaurant without too much concern.

A child who uses the toilet consistently at home is ready for travel, but with a few stipulations:

- Don't make her wait. At this age, she does not have total control over her bladder. Telling her to "hold it" won't be much good because physically, she's not there yet.
- Take the opportunity. Before leaving the apartment, before touring the museum, after she's done eating, any time you pass a public toilet, ask her to try.
- Take the initiative. Don't ask her if she "has to go;" tell her it is time to try.
- Slow down. One key to successful potty training on the road is to never be in a hurry. If this means you show up painfully early for a train, flight, or theater production, do it. This gives you ample time for stops.
- Find the WCs. In many countries, public toilets are difficult to find. Do not assume every eatery or bistro

148

has a WC available—not even for your adorable toddler. Keep ample coins in your pocket, as most public facilities (the good ones) are only for paying customers.

# When Not to Potty Train

### During flights

While I discourage the use of pull-ups during the potty training process, sometimes items such as these are necessary during travel. Other alternatives include cloth diapers with a waterproof outer lining. This will prevent any wetness from soaking into the airline seat. If she does wet in the pull-ups don't make a big deal about it. That's why you've put them on her.

*Caution: only use pull-ups when absolutely necessary. It is easy to undo many hours of training by overuse of disposable underpants.

### When there's no escape

Examples:

- When you are climbing to the cupola of a duomo with the trainee in a backpack
- When you are exploring catacombs
- When you are riding camels
- When you are on a tour of the world's largest ice cave

# When You Can Potty Train

- In the museum
- At the restaurant
- In the archaeological park

Stipulations:

**Do not disturb.** Do not potty train when it will be a huge disruption to other people. For example, a theater production is probably not the best place. Yes, you can ask the entire row of people to stand up in order to let you fumble your way to the aisle, but this is not ideal. Unless you are at Lion King, with a largely sympathetic audience, refrain from potty training during these special events.

**Mark your territory (figuratively).** It is possible to potty train in a public place, such as a restaurant, but as soon as you enter the building, find the restroom. If you are in a large building, such a museum, open up the map and mark where the bathrooms are. Plan your route so that you can see a few things and easily make a restroom break.

**Don't Get Distracted.** Viewing art and artifacts is extremely engrossing. But as the parent of a toilet training toddler, you must be vigilant regarding your child's physical cues. Keep good track of the time between breaks, and watch for tell-tale potty break signs: agitation, knees-together dancing, or physical holding.

**Get cleaned up.** Always pack a simple cleanup kit. This should include a change of pants, wet wipes, a few paper towels, and a baggie (to put the soiled items in). Never leave home without it.

**Remain Calm.** You may be embarrassed, hurt, or even angry, when your child has an accident, but she will calm down much more quickly if you stay calm. Even if you feel she has deliberately done it to get your attention, you must downplay it. The less reaction she gets from you for the unsavory behavior the better.

# CHAPTER 15: OUTSMARTING YOUR TODDLER 101

## The Gypsy Mama Basics or Out Smarting Your Toddler 101

Couple insatiable curiosity with an ever expanding world and you have a recipe for endless toddler distraction. One day, you look down, and at your feet is a two or three foot tall barbarian in place of the happy-go-lucky baby you had last week.

He doesn't MEAN to be a barbarian, it's simply the byproduct of lightning fast brain connections being made around the clock and processing new experiences faster than a super computer. There are so many new things to try and taste and climb and wonder about; no wonder toddlers are all over the place!

What some parents fail to realize is that this stage of child development is not "the terrible twos" (so named by someone who'd not yet had a THREE year old). Rather it's the TERRIFIC twos, and threes, only made better by the fabulous fours!

As with most things in life, attitude is EVERYTHING.

A parent who looks at this stage of rapid brain and motor skill growth as, not a storm to be weathered, but an opportunity to provide her child with the foundation of excellent habits upon which to build his future, will find a thousand tiny ways to give her child the skills he needs to explore the world and become a life long learner. We call these the "Gypsy Mama Basics."

## What Gypsy Mamas Know

The Gypsy Mama knows a few things that the average Mama might not.

She knows that her child's ever frustrating toddler moments are actually a gift and an opportunity.

- She knows that what appears as a challenge to her authority is actually emerging independence that needs to be nurtured, and a search for the boundaries around her toddler's life.
- She knows that her role as Gypsy Mama is to quietly guide her protege, introduce him to the world, channel his curiosity and give him the skills to work within the boundaries that life creates around him.
- She views each day as an opportunity, each difficulty as a teachable moment and each lesson as an adventure and a game.
- She is calm and focused, and she gracefully rises above the fray.
- She also has a few secret weapons in her bag of tricks.

## The 7 P's, Once Again!

Remember my Uncle Dick and his seven P's?

Proper Prior Planning Prevents Piss Poor Performance!

**Nowhere is this more true than in wrangling a toddler. The Gyspy Mama is an expert at planning in advance for virtually every eventuality and those she can't plan for, she's considered her reaction to in advance.**

Most power struggles and meltdowns with toddlers can be avoided (or at very least minimized significantly) by deciding ahead of time what your reaction will be in a less than ideal situation.

The Gypsy Mama plans the museum visit for the time of day that Junior is most amiable; her secondary level of planning involves a strategy for what she will do "just in case" the worst happens.

What is the worst? Depends on your kid... a potty accident? A temper tantrum? Refusal to eat? Running away?

The Gypsy Mama arrives prepared, scouts bathrooms and exits ahead of time, and has practiced her deep cleansing breaths and her serene smile, so if she must race from the building, screaming toddler under her arm like a football, she will, at least, do so gracefully without ruining HER day, even if it ruins Junior's.

The "take home message" of Uncle Dick's Seven P's for Gypsy Mamas?

Think ahead, teach at home, plan your reactions, and stay calm!

## Gypsy Mama Moves To Start At Home

The BEST Gypsy Mamas are always thinking about what they can teach at home that will serve them well on the road. Here are a few examples of what you can teach your child:

**In the grocery store that applies to the airport...**

**How to hold the cart** and walk calmly up and down the aisles... which translates to holding the stroller, or luggage cart, or the hem of your dress and walking calmly through the airport. For our family, we used the phrase "hand on cart," so the toddler would immediately know what to do. Both grocery stores and airports can be congested, which means you can safely develop the child's skill of following you through a crowd.

**How to carry his own bag**, filled with a loaf of bread, instead of a teddy bear... which translates to a little backpack carry-on. Upon entering the store, allow your child to carry a small basket, and as you walk through the store, tell him which items to 'pack.'

**How to place things out of his own bag onto the conveyor belt**, which translates to the security checkpoints at the airport. When you reach the check-out, allow him to put the items he has collected onto the conveyor.

Each of these things gives your toddler appropriate portions of independence while teaching valuable travel skills.

**In the restaurant that applies to EVERYTHING...**

**How to sit quietly and wait for his food.** You'll thank yourself a million times for working on that one.

Some strategies:

• Bring your own crayons

155

- DON'T bring noisy toys... a felt book is a good choice
- DON'T let your child play with (or lick) items on the table. Seriously, we've seen kids licking the tops of powdered cheese or salt containers. We also knew parents who let their toddlers chew up the sugar packets while waiting, and this does NOT encourage the long term behavior you're seeking to develop, nor does it take into consideration those who came before, or after you. Licking? No.
- Include your child in conversation, even as a toddler.
- Bring a book and read quietly aloud.
- Use an 'inside voice,' which is different from whispering and worlds away from an 'outside voice.'
- DON'T hit, kick, or otherwise disturb the table.
- DO give your toddler an either/or choice regarding food.
- DO allow your child, if she's able, to order her own food, remembering proper respectful words. *If you are in a foreign country, encourage her to use the words of that language, as it will help prevent shyness about speaking in a second language.
- DO begin by choosing an informal restaurant (where screaming fits don't stand out so much), and this does not have to be a place where food comes in cardboard boxes. Look instead for a family-friendly place where people actually come to your table to take your order.
- DO move to more formal places once you have practiced a little. By age three, our kids could behave well at any restaurant, even ones with 'fancy' tablecloths and lit candles. Believe me, it is possible for your toddler to be more well-behaved at an expensive restaurant than older children--it is all in the preparation and training.

**How to fold his hands and show patience.** Which is often necessary whilst waiting on late planes, or buses, or on long car rides to visit Grandma. Teach the following

156

rhyme (that every preschool teacher knows and swears by!) while open ng and closing your hands in time to the rhyme:

"Open, shut them, Open, shut them, give a little clap! Open, shut them, Open, shut them, fold them in your lap!"

**Folding hands** (and the ability to do so when told) will give your toddler a social leg up on his peers and increase the freedom you have to experience new things together. We instruct our toddlers to fold their hands upon entering a store with breakable things, in the museum, on the sofa at a new friend's house who has not necessarily "child proofed" the room, while waiting for a meal in a restaurant, and when the temptation to yank a sister's braid has just become too much. "Fold your hands and show self control," are words to work into your Gypsy Mama toolkit.

Taking your toddler to the restaurant will allow her bits of independence, while she learns useful skills, such as patience, following directions, making choices, speaking clearly, sitting still, and appropriately entertaining herself. So don't be afraid! Take your toddler out for dinner!

In the library that applies to hotel lobbies...

**To use a "library voice,"** which will make your toddler a welcome wonder to the staff of the upscale hotel you visit in Paris.

**To be gentle with a book** or magazine that does not belong to her. Many times I have seen toddlers ripping magazines to shreds, while the mother shrugs her shoulders and gives the "toddlers will be toddlers" look. Don't fall into this mindset. Believe it or not, toddlers can learn to be gentle.

**To sit quietly with a book.** Start with five minutes and one book.  Work up to thirty minutes (by age three and a half or four) and a couple of books. As your child develops the ability to focus and extend her attention span, her ability to pick up details will develop as will her patience in doctor's offices, airports, and embassy waiting rooms--to say nothing of the value of increasing literacy!

## Keri Says:

When we first brought our toddlers to the museum, we quickly realized they were frequently distracted or excited and would forget to keep their hands folded.

So, the Wellman kids had 3 options: to hold the hand of a parent or older sibling, to keep their hands clasped behind their backs, or put their hands inside their pockets. This habit has alleviated the fears of many a security guard in the finest museums of Europe.

While we began practicing museum etiquette years ago while doing everyday shopping, to our chagrin today, upon entering a 'breakables' store, our kids will now remind their siblings: "Pretend you're in a museum."

**At the local museum that applies to the L'Ouvre...**

No one in their right mind jumps into the deep end of a pool without having first learned to swim where he can touch. Likewise, your toddler should have the opportunity to learn to swim in the local museum before spending a long day in the L'Ouvre, or Smithsonian.

**The Children's Museum**: learn to explore, share and consider the needs of those coming before and after you.

**The Science Museum**: learn to look, and listen, and ask questions... in your library voice, of course.

**The Art Museum**: learn to identify a few favorites, identify colors, textures and shapes, learn to use your EYES not your FINGERS.

A useful travel skill for museums, especially if you have more than one child, is to teach "single-file." Museum exhibits are often crowded, but your child can learn to follow you single file, so as not to be in the way of other people.

In addition, the local museum is a perfect place for learning to wait your turn. Toddlers are notoriously impatient, but you can help your child expand his capacity by practicing patience at the local museum. Through practice, he will learn that his questions will be answered and he will get to see everything in time.

## Bum Spots

This is not a disease, it's a trick I discovered when I had two four year olds, a two year old and a baby and going ANYWHERE was a goat rodeo.

At the time IKEA was selling these little round woven chair pads in bright colors, just the right size for a little bum. I let the kids pick out one in their favorite colour and then convinced them that they were the BEST place to sit while watching movies at home, while listening to stories before bedtime and when coloring before lunch. In this way the children were quickly trained to believe that their "bum spots" were the BEST place to hang out and have fun.

On the day I was set to donate blood, I loaded up the kids and tested my theory. I tossed the bum spots out around the edge of the clinic and the munchkins plopped down and, to the amazement of the nurses, didn't move an inch for a full thirty minutes.

159

For the next several years those bum spots saw a LOT of use: libraries for story hour, doctor's offices when I didn't want them touching nasty infectious toys, ferry waiting rooms, in great-grandma's nursing home, family reunions and more.

## Hands On The Wall

More than once we've reduced strangers to giggles when they come upon our family at the counter of a fast food restaurant and find four little people with both hands flat against the wall (or counter) with their feet slightly spread.

They look like little convicts, lined up for a police pat down. In fact, what they are doing is exercising self control and remaining in ONE SPOT long enough for Mama to turn her attention to something else for thirty seconds without wondering what the herd is up to!

We came upon the idea when our second child was born and we had to get one kid out of the vehicle, then turn our backs to get the baby.

**"Put your hands on the car/wall,"** is one of those phrases that will turn out to be SO handy if you teach your child to obey instantly. Make a game out of it at first, seeing how fast your child can comply and rewarding them handsomely.

For years our kids were automatically trained to get out of the car and put their hands on the back quarter panel while they waited for us to collect the baby, stroller, or whatever else we needed before heading into the grocery store.

The ability to keep out of traffic in the parking lot is a health and safety consideration! We used "Hands on the Wall!" for restaurants, waiting in train terminals while tickets were being ordered, waiting on grandparents who were taking a little longer than the toddlers liked in public places and any other time when we needed little people to STOP and be STILL for a few minutes. Just for fun, I tried this on my teenagers this week... it still works!

## Our toddler nightmares and what we learned

**Fresh Fruit Folly:**

After a six hour flight, I was spending a four hour layover in Chicago with my kindergartner, preschooler, toddler and baby. Having just arrived from a place covered with four feet of snow for nine months of the year, we were thrilled to discover containers of full-flavored fresh fruit at the airport.

Oblivious to certain facts of nature regarding the effects of fresh fruit on toddlers, I let him have his fill. In fact, I thought it amusing the vast quantity of fruit he consumed during our layover. But fresh fruit is healthy, right?

Half an hour into our 45 minute connecting flight, I smelled something. I looked over at my toddler, but he was sleeping peacefully, and the wretched smell was not coming from the baby in my arms either. I eyed the nearby WC suspiciously, wondering what kind of airline would allow such an odor to persist.

Upon landing, my toddler awoke and proceeded to horrify me with one word: "Yuck!"

He kept repeating the word over and over...I calmly waited until everyone else was off the plane, then I grabbed the toddler's hand and led him and the troops to the nearest facilities.

We had a containment leak of Chernobyl proportions. Fortunately, I had my clean-up kit handy. By the time grandpa was tossing him in the air, no one would have guessed what had happened only minutes before.

161

By staying calm and being prepared, I was able to handle the situation without a lot of stress; in fact, my toddler didn't even cry, he just kept saying "yuck," which was embarrassing at the time, but funny now.

I also learned the impact of large amounts of fruit on a toddler's digestive system--I never made that mistake again.

**Green Mountain Boy... and we're not talking Ethan Allen here!**

We had the great fortune, for several years, to live at the edge of the White Mountains in northern New Hampshire. It was one of those idyllic seasons of life that was marked by postcard like snapshots of young family life in the forest.

For the first time in a decade we were closer than a thousand miles from the Grandparents. We took advantage of that novelty by regularly making the seven hour drive to Canada for a visit, a pilgrimage which wound through the pristine Green Mountains of Vermont and out onto the flatlands of Quebec.

You'd think that the fourth child born into a nomadic family would be born with his boots on and immune to the usual travel challenges. Not so. Ezra was born with an unfortunate propensity to toss his cookies anytime we were in the car for more than a quick ride about town. Add the curvy, twisty, two lane mountain roads and you have a recipe for disaster.

I tried everything, feeding him lightly, moving him to a seat closer to the front, ginger candies, ginger ale, homeopathic remedies, pressure bands, all of it, except the anti-nausea drugs that he was too little for. The kid is just a puker.

He's eight now. I'd love to say he got over it. He didn't. Poor elf puked his way through the high Sierra Madre that run the length of central Mexico and down into Guatemala this past winter. He takes the "Drama-immune" (what he calls Dramamine) now and that helps somewhat, but not enough.

What did I learn? Long suffering, the value of anti-bacterial wipes and to make the kid wear a plastic scoop bib until we hit the border.

The moral of the story: work with what you've got, remember the 7 P's and pack your sense of humor.

163

# SECTION FOUR

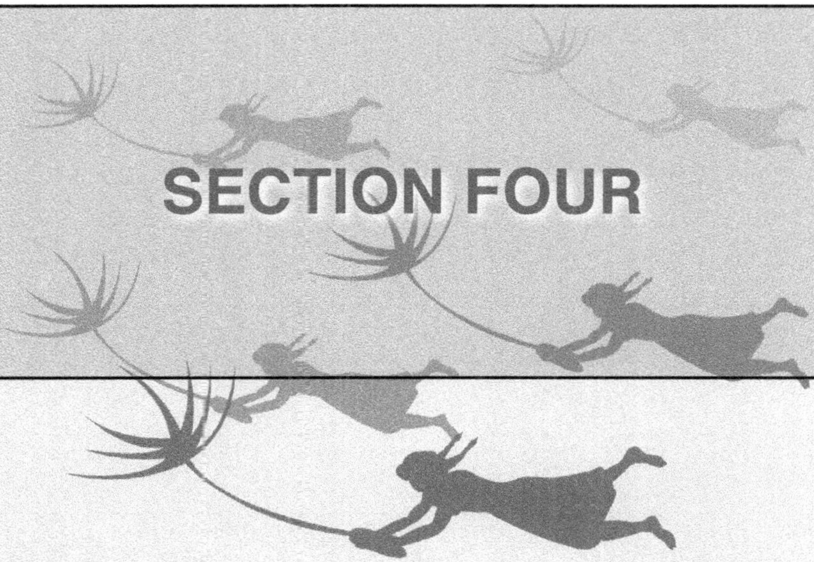

# TRAVEL WITH SCHOOL-AGERS

# CHAPTER 16: INTRO TO SCHOOL AGE TRAVEL

Well, parents, it's time to pat yourselves on the back! Raise a glass to a job well-done! You have survived months, and perhaps even years of sleep deprivation; made it through bottles, diapers, potty training and tantrums; have dealt with screaming and crying and outright disobedient toddlers; and now the fun begins—the school aged years. It's going to be an adventure!

Take a good look at that kid sitting at the table coloring. His brain has now formed trillions of neural networks. Complex emotions, such as empathy and envy, have begun to develop and will continue to do so until around age ten. His vocabulary has expanded drastically from the time he first muttered "dada;" and his capacity to acquire language is at its greatest. You may have noticed the radical development of gross motor skills, such as balance and coordination, and fine motor skills, such as handling a crayon or paintbrush or violin bow.

There is not a computer on earth that has such complex wiring or capacity for information as your child's mind. Yet with all of this information going into the brain, sometimes the output is still less than desirable. As Dickens' famous opening line explains...

*"It was the best of times, it was the worst of times, it was the age of wisdom, it was the age of foolishness..."*

**I am fairly certain Dickens was talking about traveling with children.**

Just because you survived babyhood and toddlerhood does not mean travel suddenly becomes easy. Quite the contrary, the challenges you now face with your child can be every bit as trying as those you faced in toddlerhood-- they are just usually more subtle.

Your child will continue to seek independence; and it is your job to give him appropriate doses of it at the right times. How you parent on the road will absolutely shape your child's view of the world.

**The best of times...**

The world is the perfect classroom, offering every subject imaginable for the mobile student: science, history, math, geography and language are just the tip of the iceberg. Each subject is out there waiting for the traveling family to take hold with both hands.

Using the world as a classroom is by far the best type of learning available for today's globally aware child. Furthermore, through the trials, challenges and adventures of travel, your family will form a bond like no other.

## The worst of times...

Talking back, eye-rolling, heavy sighs, yelling: whichever tool your child chooses to wield against your authority, you must make plans to deal with the behavior before it happens. When you travel, life is compacted into a space and time continuum so small, it could fit into the overhead luggage bin with your carry-on: emotions run higher, children push boundaries further; and yet, your hearts can draw closer than you'd ever imagined.

As your child asserts his independence, you must walk a fine line. It is not always easy to know what to do in a particular situation—and if your angelic child suddenly ignores you and wanders off in that crowded marketplace, you have to be prepared to respond accordingly.

To give independence is a frightening thing, but if you train your child to be a savvy traveler, you can give him the space he needs, even when you are on the road together.

## The age of wisdom...

Your child is now capable of learning much about his world, and he has the neurological capacity to master important behaviors such as self-control and good decision-making. When you set up your child for successful travel through proper training, you will be in awe when you see him making wise choices.

## The age of foolishness...

A lot is going on in your child's brain, and sometimes even the most well-prepared child lapses. Making mistakes is a natural part of life; and let's face it--some children will only learn the hard way. It makes your job challenging as a parent, but it is not impossible to deal with while traveling.

In fact, the most hard-headed kids are often the most consistent once a lesson is learned. They are the decision-makers and the ones who take charge—these are the children who usually make instant friends with kids at the park—even when they don't speak the same language. And yet, foolish mistakes will be made. It is your job to prevent them if possible, but prepare for them when they do occur.

## The Possibility of Big Time Travel

For many families, middle childhood is the perfect time to launch out on the adventure of a lifetime. Perhaps you backpacked around Asia in your early twenties and have dreams of returning to the temples at Ankor Wat with your children. Or perhaps, like me, your childhood included major travel and you'd like to continue that multi-generational vision of developing world citizens with your own children.

Whatever the motivator, be encouraged, THIS is the perfect time to take a year, or ten, and do something truly fabulous with your kids.

**Jenn Says:**

Middle child-hood is a GREAT time to travel. Sure, there are added challenges as your child "grows a brain" and begins to express his own unique thoughts, desires and emotions. But the flip side is that the entire world opens up and there is great delight in exploring, learning and adventuring together. From my perspective, this stage of childhood represents "Mama Nirvana"--everyone is toilet trained and no one is driving! It is the PERFECT time to hit the road as a family!

# CHAPTER 17: SAFETY PLANS

## Safety Plans For Independent Children

Once your child is out of a stroller and walking on his own, travel gets MUCH easier. No need to struggle with strollers on less than accessible train platforms, no need to carry your little person in a sling or backpack in addition to the carry-on bags you're already lugging, in fact, now your little traveler is carrying his own little bag.

With increased mobility and increased freedom comes the need for defined boundaries and safety nets in place. Even the most responsible, attentive child can get lost in a crowd, or jostled off of a train by himself. As your children gain independence, it is vital that you put some safety measures in place.

### ID Tags

From the time our children could get out of the stroller to walk even part of a day out, I tagged them.

Simple tags with their photo, name, and pertinent contact information, such as the name and address of the hotel we were staying at and our cell phone number. I printed these on card stock and slid them into conference ID tag holders that clipped to the children's clothing.

I know there is some debate about printing a child's name on anything he carries, but we minimized the risk of these tags being used to lure our children away by using a small font (too small to read unless you were quite close to the tag) and by clipping the tag so that the printed side faced the child's body and the blank side was out.

That kid we lost in the market... he was tagged. My only consolation in the sheer panic of that moment was that he could be returned to our hotel by anyone who found him, and that our cell number was on the tag too.

**Safety Plans**

Every time we enter a metro station one of my children will loudly announce the memorized safety plan:

"If we get lost, we sit right down where we are and we wait. You will come back for us. If we get left on the train platform, we sit on the nearest bench and we wait. You will catch the next train back and get us. If we get left ON the train, we go to the next stop, get off, and sit on the nearest bench. You will come get us."

The take home message: "You will come back and get us."

**Our kids are very sure that we will ALWAYS come for them and so they can sit confidently and wait.**

We've never lost a kid on a train, but we did lose Grandma once, in Washington D.C. The kids were freaking out because they hadn't told Grandma the plan! How would she know what to do?!

It is important to have a plan. Memorize it. Stick to it.

**Passwords**

We have, on occasion, found ourselves traveling with a bigger group of families for a week long field trip. Sometimes the kids don't know all of the adults in the group

172

well and so we devised a password system to help the children identify the "safe" adults.

Should a child become lost when we're traveling with a group, we have a prearranged password that all of the children have memorized.

If they are lost and an adult they don't know comes to get them, that adult must know the password. In this way the children can be confident that they are going to rejoin our group with a safe person, and the parents can be confident that their child will not be lured away by someone less than safe.

**Two Way Radios & Cell Phones**

As our children have gotten older and we've traveled more, there are occasions when we will leave them alone for a short period of time, in a hotel room, such as when we're downstairs in a hotel at a business dinner after bedtime.

It was my husband's genius idea to invest in two way radios for this purpose. One radio goes with Mom and Dad, one radio stays with the oldest child. The kids watch their movie, brush their teeth and go to bed while Mom and Dad get an evening out within easy reach of the radios.

Cell phones could also be used, but having two cell phones activated as you travel from country to country can become expensive and inconvenient. The radios work everywhere, so long as we have batteries.

The radios have extended the freedom of our older children, allowing them to go together (our kids always go in a group when they're out and about without us) to the park, or the library, or the corner store, while knowing that they can be called back at any time and, more importantly, that they can call US if they need anything.

Our son was recently given a military issue radio with a larger range and a GPS built in. We plan to get a second one like this, which will have the added benefit of GPS coordinates so we'll know EXACTLY where the kids are and be able to walk to them if we need to. I can see the benefits of this with teenagers! :)

## Lost & Found

It occurred to us recently that our kids needed to know what to do if, in a foreign country, they suddenly found themselves alone for some reason.

Tragedy does strike occasionally, and fortune favors the prepared.

We are in the process of working through an emergency plan for our older children (ten and up) that will give them the tools they need to contact an embassy, get in touch with relatives at home, access the money they need in the meantime, and make the contacts they need to be rescued.

I hope we never need that plan, but if we ever DO, I feel much better as a mother knowing that my big kids have the skills to get themselves the help they need and get home.

Consider that carefully as you travel with your children, make contingency plans, prepare for the worst, and then expect the very best.

# CHAPTER 18: PREPARING TO TRAVEL

## Getting The Kids Involved

Getting the kids involved in the planning, the packing and the process is the key to having your herd be excited and on board rather than reluctant and nervous. Roll those maps out on the dining room table and dream about far off exotic locations together.

Show the kids how far it is to different places: where Dad works, where Grandma lives, where Mom is going for her business conference, where the stops on your Round The World plane ticket are!

**Involving the kids in the planning accomplishes several things:**

- It lets them feel part of the process instead of like an extra piece of baggage.
- It gives them some power, a vote, some measure of independence.
- It teaches them how to plan a trip--an important life skill!
- They learn how to read maps, which is a skill sorely lacking in many grown-ups!

Letting your kids help pack and plan teaches them much about real life and big dreams.

Dreaming out loud with our children is one of the most useful and most bonding things we've incorporated into family life. It is great for kids to see that parents have hopes and dreams too; and it's absolutely necessary to teach them how to put boots to those dreams and give them the tools to do anything in life they choose to.

As a family you'll learn that "you can have anything you want, but you can't have everything at once," and you'll practice working hard toward a goal, making something happen, and focusing on what you REALLY WANT, one thing at a time.

It took us two years of dedicated effort to make our dream of intercontinental cycling a reality. Even if we'd never taken the trip, the process of dreaming and planning and working together with our kids would have been worth all of the effort.

## Map It

If you have a home base, hang a map on the wall and let the kids stick pins or stickers on the places you've been. We use a color code system: gold stars for places we've been, blue stars for places where loved ones live, and green stars for places we'd like to go. It gives the kids a real visual on distances and geography, as well as expanding their imaginations. The more stickers you apply, the smaller the world begins to appear.

## Wish List

If you are in the planning stages of a trip, have the kids to make a "dream list" of places they would like to go. If they have done a bit of traveling, they may have some clear ideas. If not, then have them list types of places or activities that interest them. Or, give them a latitude or longitude on the globe and see what they come up with.

Even if you don't end up choosing one of their destinations, it is a great way for the child to learn some geography and

176

to spark their imaginations; because in today's world, it is truly possible for them to go far.

## Do Your Homework

When we travel, there are certain things we learn in country but other things we learn ahead of time. The things my kids remember most are the things they have researched.

If your child can read, then he can do research prior to travel. It is as simple as finding a book, encyclopedia, or doing a basic internet search to find out about a location.

We have our kids do research and then give a presentation on what they found. They begin by asking the famous 5 W's: who, what, why, when and where. These questions can be asked on two scales: the grand "world famous" scale, and on the smaller "local" scale. Regional stories are often MUCH more interesting and enlightening. If you can find local stories before you go, it will give your child an "ah-ha!" moment worthy of a Sherlock Holmes story when you run across the character or event while in country.

A few questions you may ask...

**Who:** Did any famous historical people come from that country? Are there any people (fictional or real) from the region in which we will be staying?

**What:** What is the country like in terms of topography or climate? What will we expect to see in our region?

**When:** When was civilization developed here? When was the current government created?

**Where:** Where is this place on the world map? Where is our village?

**Why:** Why is this an important place in the world? Why do we want to go there?

Regional characters are most interesting if you can find them. Once you learn of a character, you can play a "Where's Waldo" of sorts during your trip. While exploring Europe we have looked for signs of Napoleon, Constantine, the Bavarian Empress Elizabeth (known as Sissy), and Charlemagne. It always amazes us when one of these characters pops up unexpectedly.

## Fun Games To Play That Prepare Your Kids For New Experiences

We've always been big on making a game out of learning new skills, and turning even the ho-hum into an adventure for our kids. When they were tiny and we were preparing to take them to exotic places for the first time, we came up with a series of games we played at home to get them ready. Even big kids have fun with these:

### Tooth Brush Drills

Perhaps the number one way people become ill when traveling is from ingesting local water that contains contaminants, or parasites, or some other ugly, microscopic critter. Remembering not to drink the water is easy.

Remembering not to rinse your toothbrush, is not. Tooth brushing is one of those things we do on autopilot, and we have to retrain ourselves NOT to use sink water when we do it.

- Randomly announce that the bathroom has been transported to Mexico, or North Africa, or Myanmar, and as such, the water is not to be trusted.
- Place a water bottle by the sink and teach your children how to rinse their tooth brushes, swish and spit using only the water in that bottle.
- Make it fun by making a loud buzzer noise if a child touches the faucet, or by announcing that the child

178

has contracted some horrible plague and must now take his medicine (make it fun medicine, this is a game!)

Our youngest child, at three, was the toothbrush police when we traveled. He'd be the one yelling loudly from the bathroom, "DON'T DRINK THE WATER!! DON'T RINSE YOUR TOOTHBRUSH!! YOU'LL BE SORRY!!!!"

## International Dinners

Many parents worry about their children's eating habits as they travel. Some children are very difficult when it comes to meal times and encouraging flexibility and dietary branching out can be a real challenge. One of the ways that we encouraged a broad palate in our children, from the time they were babies, was to have an international dinner at least once a week.

- Choose a country head to the library (or search on line) for recipes native to that place.
- Shop for the foods and do the cooking together with your kids.
- Decorate the table with a map of that country, or a drawing of the flag your child makes.
- Find some music from that country to play, and maybe a story book about life there, or the mythology of the culture.
- Don't just introduce a new food, introduce a new people, place, and type of life experience.

These are the tiny steps that are easy to take in world schooling our children without ever leaving home.

We often tried to schedule the international dinners to coincide with evenings when we were having guests for dinner. Other families are often eager to join the party and bring something they've learned about that country to share. If you can find an actual PERSON to invite to dinner (or perhaps even cook with your family) so much the better!

The goal of this game is to make foreign people, places and their foods less scary to skeptical little people.

One more note... this is a great way to introduce the concept of the "No Thank You Bite" we discussed in the chapter on food and picky eaters.

It is certainly fine for kids, and adults, to prefer some foods over others, and no child need eat a whole plate of lima beans if they truly dislike them. However, taking one bite of something before passing judgement on it is a requirement at our house.

There are cultures in which refusing food is the height of rudeness and our children need to be prepared to honor their hosts, be grateful for what is set before them, and try anything. Besides, sometimes they find that the slimy looking green stuff on top of their tacos (*nopales*-cactus paddle) is actually their new favorite thing!

## Keri Says:

If you don't have time to prep an international dinner, at least try to pick up a food that is out of the ordinary for your family once a week. In the Wellman house, our kids have dubbed this "Weird Food Night." No matter how much I discourage the word "weird," the name has endured.

The rules: They must take one big bite of the new food. After their one bite is taken, they can forgo the food entirely but without snacks afterwards. Don't let the kids graze prior to dinner, because hungry kids are MUCH more likely to enjoy food that seems "weird" to them.

## Power Free Evenings

We're a pretty plugged in society, in general. Rare is the household that doesn't have a TV, game console, ipods, computers, DVD players or some configuration thereof. Some families have one of each in every child's room. Kids who are used to so much electronic entertainment may have difficulty unplugging while on the road and declare themselves "bored" fairly quickly.

I am in NO WAY anti-media. But I am definitely in favor of the judicious use of it.

Our kids enjoy a movie night as much as anyone. They each have their own ipod. We have six computers in a family of six people. But we're not emotionally dependent on these things for our happiness, or for contentment in the car, or at home, or anywhere else.

Unplugging once in a while has its merits, especially for children who need to develop a whole range of coping mechanisms for the rest of their lives. Self entertainment and the ability to be content with very little is not a small thing, and is relatively easily accomplished, simply by adhering to the "less is more" philosophy of stuff and tech time for kids.

Good friends of ours practice this with "power free evenings" once a week.

Every Friday afternoon at around 4 p.m. they unplug everything in the house but the fridge.

- They light candles for dinner, play board games after dinner, read aloud from a good book, color, paint, play dominoes, put on plays for one another... anything and everything that does not require an electrical outlet to enjoy it.

- This is a GREAT strategy for preparing children to travel to places where there may or may not be reliable electricity--or any electricity at all.

When our power was cut for three days in Africa, the children just assumed we were playing an extended game of "Power Free Evenings" and we had a lot of fun.

## No Toys Allowed

Whether you are hiking to your favorite picnic spot in the woods, spending the day on the shores of a lake, or sunning yourself on the beach, try leaving all toys at home. This encourages kids to use their imaginations and make do with what is around them.

One of our kids created a game called "Kingdom Building" and is always on the lookout for a good pile of rocks to build his castles. With sticks for people and rocks for building material, what more could a kid want?

## Bathroom Fun

Children are notoriously amused by bathrooms, at home and abroad. I'll never forget my oldest son's first encounter with a bidet in Mexico City or the slightly disturbed and violated look on his face after attempting to use it for the first time! We never quite got over the jokes about squatties in southern Italy and Africa... but then, we have three boys.

In our usual vein of "let's prepare them at home before being embarrassed abroad," we practiced for "different" bathrooms at home.  How? By posting a sign that informed users the bathroom was now in Germany and no one could use it without paying fifty cents, or Mexico and in order to get a few sheets of toilet paper one would need to pay a quarter to whichever family member had been designated the keeper of the toilet paper.

If you want to get really "authentic," take the toilet paper out altogether and put a plastic coke bottle with a hole drilled in the cap by the toilet filled with water... portable bidet like we saw over and over in Tunisia.

This game is the MOST fun if you wait to play it until you have friends over for the day!

# CHAPTER 19: LIFE ON THE ROAD

## Game Plans: Practical Strategies for Traveling with Kids

While it is beneficial to take time to explain your decisions with your child, there are critical moments in travel when children simply must obey. This means, no counting to three, no negotiating, and no talking back.

Though your child may be mature beyond her years, there are times when children seem to gravitate unwittingly towards a dangerous situation.

It is the parents' job, as leaders of the travel team, to build a trusting relationship with the other team members, so that when critical situations arise, the children obey immediately.

### Halt!

Remember this game from the toddler chapters? When we travel, this is perhaps the most utilized word in our vocabulary. Very simply, the child must freeze in his tracks the moment he hears the word. When our children were toddlers it was merely a fun game, now during the school age years (and teen years) it has become a valuable reflex. Countless times, the word "halt" has made our journeys easier and safer. When a car ran a red light as we were crossing a street in Prague, the word "halt," which I uttered with enough force to shake St. Vittus cathedral, saved my oldest child's life.

When we travel, we give our children age-appropriate autonomy. However, children are easily distracted and wander into danger. They might be watching traffic one second when they suddenly reach out to pick up a pigeon feather from the gutter. A split second of distraction is enough to lead to tragedy. Therefore, it is vital children learn to "stop" on command.

Our philosophy is obey first, discuss later. Because we have spent years building trust within our team, our children know that when they obey, they will soon know the reason why. They understand that our commands are not formed because we get some twisted satisfaction from being domineering.

Travel can be dangerous, but travel trained children are not fearful because they trust the rules have value.

**Against the Wall**

The second most useful command in our vocabulary is "against the wall."

Because we travel with four children, which we sometimes describe as "herding chickens," having the kids line up against a wall is a necessity. When we exit a train or subway, having the children line up against the wall does several things:

- First we can make sure everyone is accounted for
- Second, it gets the children out of the way of other passengers
- Third, it gives us time to get our bearings

You can "anchor" the children by having them place a hand against the wall, or simply have them line up with their backs against it (if the wall isn't too grimy).

## Single File

For their own safety and so they are not an annoyance to other travelers, our children have been taught "single file."

This is very useful when using mass transit, when in museums, or when working your way through a crowd. It keeps the child from getting run over by other people, and it keeps other people from being tripped by a daydreaming seven year-old.

## Sibling Groups, or "The Buddy System"

Your family dynamics will determine in what order your children do any task. If you have two older children, they may be allowed to go off by themselves in a particular setting and rendezvous with you at a set point and time.

If you are lining up the children to board a flight or train, you will line them up according to who will sit next to whom. Make the decision beforehand to avoid cries of "but you sat next to him last time!"

Ideally, one parent boards first, followed by the child who will sit next to the window, followed by his travel buddy, followed by the next travel team, while the last parent brings up the rear.

Relationships between siblings develop and change as the years go by. For a while, my two oldest could not sit next to each other without one of them screaming (not ideal for travel). During another stretch of time, my two boys could not sit next to each other without wrestling. For a few months, my oldest daughter began mothering her younger brother, which caused a riotous outbreak of rebellion. To make travel more convenient for you and to keep your sanity, make the decisions and assign "Buddies" well ahead of time.

Assigning travel buddies makes kids a little safer, it helps smooth the flow of the travel day, but it also provides a wonderful opportunity for two children to work on building their relationship and celebrate some "special time" together. Both of our families have four kids, so the opportunity for two siblings to share some bonding time while they're buddies is priceless!

Ideally, one parent boards first, followed by the child who will sit next to the window, followed by his travel buddy, followed by the next travel team, while the last parent brings up the rear.

## Line Up

While it is important to consider current family dynamics when making seating arrangements, it is equally important you develop a set order of operations that overrides personal preferences in case of emergencies.

Our default mode (in critical situations) is to have the children line up from youngest to oldest. When we say "line up," they will automatically do so in that order, regardless of current emotional states.

Again, you will not always have time to explain your actions during travel, and it is imperative the children are trained to react quickly to orders so they can remain safe and calm.

## Obey first, discuss later.

If the commands and training sound a bit Machiavellian to you, remember this: if you wish to enjoy traveling with your children, you must equip them to handle the pressures they will face as part of the travel team.

Every football team has a coach with a play book. The team practices until the maneuvers become intuitive. No one knows exactly how the game will play out, but every team member has been prepared to handle a wide variety of situations.

Your children do not have to be little soldiers, but they do have to be well-trained members of the team.

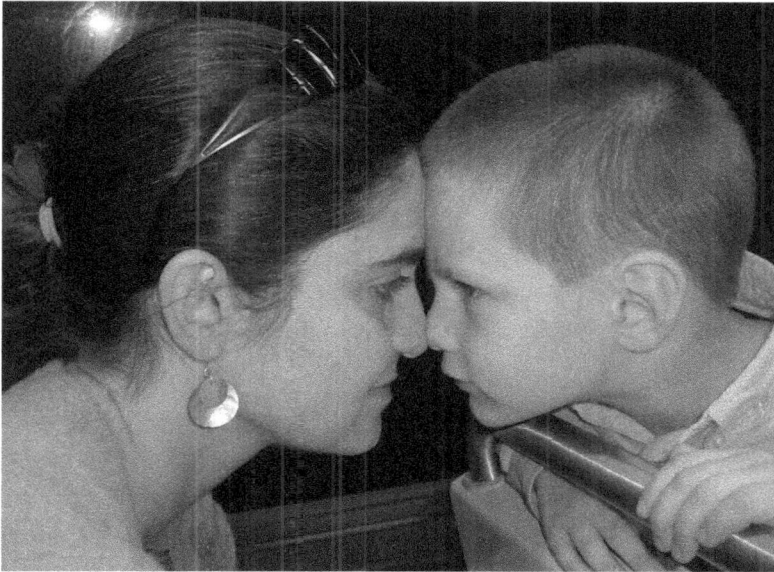

## Crime and Punishment

It would be wonderful if I could give you a sure-fire method that would change your child's heart and soul so she would never misbehave again. However, no one knows your child like you.

Some consequences are not "one size fits all." In our family, a simple conference will bring one child to tears and repentance, while another must have all privileges removed to leave the slightest impression on his conscience.

On the road rule-breaking is even more challenging because you are not in a routine environment. Saying, "Be good or we won't take you to the mall," is much different than, "Be good or we won't take you to the Mayan temple!" If you have spent the time and money to get the family safely to a country that has a Mayan Temple, then everyone is going-- and your child knows it. Punishments

189

that work at home cannot be stenciled neatly onto the travel itinerary.

Swift and pertinent consequences in childhood prevent the residual buildup of more devastating ones later. During travel, where many variables come into play, quick and logical consequences are even more crucial.

That's wonderful in theory, but how does a family put the idea of logical consequences into practice during travel, when the stakes are higher? What if one child pushes another while "helping" him up the steps in the catacombs; or if one child shouts in the cathedral, next to the "quiet please" sign?

Just as our family has default commands, we also have a default consequence known as "Nose Against the Wall." It is a public time-out that can be done anywhere. If your little culprit, like ours, cheerfully points out, "There are no walls," you can rename this, "Nose Against the Pillar," "Nose Against the Tree," "Nose Against the Aqueduct," or whichever stationary object seems applicable.

"Nose against the wall" gives the travel team leaders time to bring the situation under control and to discuss further consequences.

- It allows us to determine if the incurrence was accidental or deliberate.
- Most importantly, it gets the behavior to stop immediately, so a calm discussion can ensue.

Most often "nose against the wall" is enough punishment in itself, and nothing further is required. If a child is not using self control or patience, then a few minutes of quiet contemplation without distraction (and a few odd stares from passersby) is adequate to redirect their behavior. After all, whining and arguing brings glares from others, usually directed towards the parents. With nose against the wall, the consequences, and the strange looks, fall squarely on the perpetrator.

Whichever consequence works best for your family, the key is to be consistent.

Do not overlook an incurs on simply because you are in public, because your child WILL test you when you are in public. Even your angel may decide to dent her halo during travel—expect it and prepare for it. It will save you worse headaches down the road.

## Making Connections With Other Kids

No matter where we are, our kids miss their friends.

When we are "home" with their "old friends" they talk non-stop about their friends in Germany and the Czech or in Canada. Right now, nestled into the shores of Lago de Atitlan, in Guatemala, they are missing their friends at home.

It is the best and worst of world travel: we meet people everywhere who we come to love and then ultimately say goodbye. Sometimes kids find it hard. We have one who cries bitterly every time we leave loved ones.

How do we, as parents, help our children manage the loss, maintain long distance relationships, and make new friends?

The answer will be slightly different for every child. It must be our life's work as parents to tie heart strings with our kids and remain in their inner circle as they grow, so they know they are loved, and that we can be trusted. In addition, by knowing their hearts, we can help them when they're sad and encourage them when they're happy.

In our experience, children seem to have fewer cultural inhibitions than we adults do. Upon arriving in a new place, the first thing we locate is the playground. Without fail our children dive into vigorous play with the local children and through a blend of their few words in the new language and pantomime, they make themselves understood and come away with new friends.

Through play groups, schools, volunteer opportunities, neighborhood events, local festivals and simple afternoon teas with other families children can be encouraged to interact as they travel, form friendships that may last a lifetime, and expand their definition of the world, and perhaps of themselves.

192

**Here are some ideas for helping your kids connect as you travel:**

- Participate in a playgroup

- Take them to the park
- Enroll at the local library for special events
- Attend religious services (if that's your thing)
- Take language lessons from a local
- Join an art or music co-op
- Do some volunteer work together
- Make a point of shopping where the locals do and introduce yourselves
- Take tiny treasures from "home" to share with kids you meet (candy, coins, balloons...)
- Slow down... take your time, don't rush, allow time to interact--in many places life runs at a more leisurely pace than we Westerners are used to.
- Check out the local school. There may be extracurricular activities your kids could join.
- Or find out if there is a local community college that offers programs for children.

In Germany, the Volkshohschule offers many classes and seminars for kids: authentic German baking, painting, and traditional arts & crafts are just a few of the many classes they offer for kids. Even if your children don't speak the local language, being in a hands-on class with the locals can teach them a lot.

What do you do now that your children, like mine, have friends all over the world and miss them ALL no matter where you are?

Here are some ideas for maintaining those precious friendships as your children grow:

- Create a website. Our kids friends follow our stories avidly and comment!
- Enroll in Skype... no cheaper way to have phone conversations or video "play dates" across continents. Our kids once jumped on the bed with their friends

(also jumping on their beds) over skype, from Africa to the USA.

- Snail mail... no matter how quick e-mail is, a real live postcard is precious. Write them.
- E-mail if each kid can send and receive e-mail morning and night (our twice a day rule) it will help them to stay close across the miles.
- Let 'em fly... as your kids get older, consider letting them go visit friends and family on their own... they're seasoned travelers, they can do it!
- Trade treasures... our kids carry tiny treasures from dear friends, and we give them in return. Certain kids are always shopping for other certain kids, and little collections of sweet things get shipped back and forth around the world.
- Remember the holidays... celebrate the holidays of your kids' friends regardless of where you are. Send cards and gifts, create your own party, and keep hearts close even when bodies can't be.

# CHAPTER 20: EDUCATIONAL OPPORTUNITIES

## Make It A Field Trip

Getting there is the easy part: Just buy a plane ticket, pack and GO!

Once You're There... What to do? What to see? How to document it?

Figuring out what to do with famously fickle school agers once you're on the ground, that's another story altogether. If you've included your kids in the planning you should have some idea of what they're interested in seeing and what they would like to experience in your new location, but don't stop there.

Every trip you take is an educational opportunity, even if it's just a Saturday to a local state park.

### How to create the instant field trip:

Do Your Homework!

### Books:

You may become so bogged down by logistics, you don't have time to prepare destination specific lesson plans. To make the trip more educational, create a book list for your child.

Guide books are invaluable, but don't limit yourself to non-fiction.

- Fiction or historical fiction are also great ways to get the kids' imaginations stirred prior to a trip.
- Biographies of important people bring historical sites alive.
- The Database of Award Winning Children's Literature allows you to search quickly for literature by historical period, cultural relevance and much more. This is a great resource for linking literature to travel!

Meaningful travel with kids means making connections between their thoughts and experience. Reading about Ancient Rome is fascinating, but actually walking the Fori Imperiali makes a connection in their minds, which will not soon be forgotten.

For my children, there is a great amount of excitement when they can see, touch, and feel a place they've previously read about.

## Movies:

Were any movies filmed on location in your travel destination? Even a fiction film with a weak plot and unrealistic dialogue has value to your pre-travel prep.

Movies are a good way to stir the imaginations. Plus, when you actually explore your destination, it will amuse you to recall the film version.

Be sure to look for foreign language films—these may offer glimpses into the culture you will soon see in person. They will also begin to tune your child's ear to the language of the place you're going!

**Internet:**

Can't find a good book or movie? Search YouTube. Likely, others have documented and posted clips from your destination of choice. Look online to see if the local tourist board has a DVD or promotional brochures available by post.

**Arts and Crafts:**

Art is one of my favorite ways to engage a child in a specific culture. If you will be attending a museum at your destination, find out which artists are featured or which artifacts are on display. Because larger museums have too many to list, pick a few that appeal to you.

Or delve into art history, noting the changes throughout the ages. I was amazed when my oldest, who was 12 at the time, noticed the artistic differences between the early and late funerary urns of the Etruscans—a fact that had completely escaped my notice.

Yes, you will learn new things while on the road, but for kids, the prep work makes it more meaningful.

Remember, you are dealing with small humans who are just developing abstract thought. So generally, the more concrete you make something, the easier it is for them to grasp.

This is why art is a powerful tool for meaningful travel. Art reflects culture and history on a single canvas—no books required. If you learn about regional art prior to travel, it will help your child to better understand a particular time and culture. Art is the best social studies project there is.

Once you arrive in your destination, you may be able to find a local artisan who can teach you the regional skill. Many countries also offer classes and workshops through schools.

Here in Germany, the local Volkshochschule offers classes for people of all ages—woodworking, art, dancing; language as well as regional crafts and baking. Not only will your child learn a new skill, it will give her yet another chance to interact with local children and pick up the language.

Alternately, purchase a copy of Teaching Geography Through Art and create some projects of your own before or after your trip!

## Documentation

### Cameras

Each child in our family upon turning seven receives a digital camera. If you want to see what travel is like through the eyes of your child, just wait until you watch the slideshow! I guarantee they will find things you miss.

Taking snapshots helps reinforce your child's memory. Out of all the shimmering gold mosaics of knights and sculptures of dragons, my 8 year-old chose to take a picture of the organ in the castle's chapel—an object that defines our little Mozart.

The great thing about digital cameras is that most have video capability. With limited video, a child can learn to film the crux of the event and cut out the dull stuff.

Still cameras and video teach children more than to smile and say cheese.

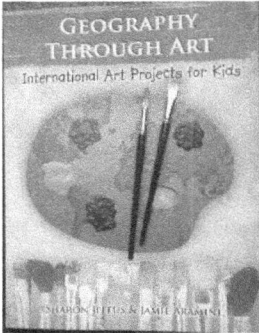

They also learn:

- Selectivity
- Discretion
- Editing
- Aesthetics
- Narrative skills

But before the cameras roll, certain ground rules must be established:

- No invading privacy
- No breaking trust
- Embarrassing photos will be deleted
- The person in the picture has the right of veto
- Failure to comply with rules results in loss of gadget

*Caution: not all cultures find it acceptable to have pictures taken. Make sure your child knows when filming is appropriate, and always make sure they ask before snapping someone's picture.

If the photos will be used on a blog or social network, make sure your child asks permission before sharing the photo with the world.

## Journaling

I love the smell of a new leather journal, but the majority of my children couldn't care less. Paper means handwriting, and handwriting means anguish. This is one case where I am all for technology.

A five year-old may not be able to write straight without a dotted blue guide line, but amazingly, she can learn to load pictures onto a blog and write a sentence about the picture.

A blog is today's journal. Even if the blog is only shared with Oma and Opa, it is a good way for a kid to document her travels and share her experiences. Plus, a blog keeps photos and information in order, so later, she can easily create a photo book for the grandparents.

If your child is under 13, you may have to set up her blog under your account (if you have one). Our family uses Wordpress, where we have both public and private blogs.

Blogs are free, easy to use, and fit in a backpack.

# CHAPTER 21: OUT OF THE MOUTHS OF BABES

**My name is Noah, and I am nine.**

Some of my favorite places I went to were Rome, Bologna, Austria, London and Paris. The things I wish I had not brought on a trip to Italy were 50 thin planks of wood called "Contraptions." I almost never used them. Instead, I liked sketching with a mechanical pencil and sketchbook. One of the titles of my sketches was "Candy Wars."

One of the best things of the trip to Italy was swimming in a big, cold, clear, scary and fun lake. I also liked riding in a motorboat. Instead of staying at home and playing video games all day, I'd rather travel around the world and explore.

**My name is Libby, and I am seven years-old.**

I have gone to Italy, London, Paris and Rome. I was born in Alaska, and I have also been to Florida.

Once I regretted bringing my little bobble-headed toy dog called a "Littlest Pet Shop" to Italy because I always lost the pieces to it, and I almost forgot one under the bed. I did like bringing my Dora the Explorer figures. They had bigger pieces than the Pet Shop. I wish I HAD brought my flippers so I could swim in Lake Garda.

If I could choose one item to bring with me for a trip, it would be a book. It would be the book called "Pippi

203

Longstockings." I really like reading it, and sometimes we don't play, so I like to read a book in that time.

My favorite place I've traveled was London and Paris. It was fun because we rented a nice hotel and there was a pizza store nearby, and we went to the very, very top of the Eiffel Tower. And one other thing--I REALLY liked the crepes there.

In London we went to a bunch of museums, and it was very interesting. I would advise to bring to a museum a notepad or a little memo book to write about the things you find interesting. And I really, really, really liked the apartment in London because it had a toy closet. We also got to go on the London Eye.

When you travel, you always have to remember if you get lost, stay where you are because if you go somewhere, and if your family comes back looking for you, they won't know where you went--and that would NOT be good.

The funnest thing I've ever done with my family is swim in Lake Garda, and that is why I wish I'd brought my flippers. And I wish I was allowed to go scuba diving. (That's why I'm jealous of Hannah Miller).

**My name is Katie. I'm 12 1/2 years old.**

Some of my favorite places I've been are the Ice Caves near Salzburg, Austria. The caves held huge glaciers of ice inside the mountain. It was cold but very beautiful. In Austria we got to go rowing on a clear lake and go on a ride called a sommerrodelbahn. It's like a slide but you go down on a small go-cart with a brake and an accelerator.

If I were going on a long trip and I could only bring one thing to entertain myself I would bring my Kindle, which is an electronic book that can hold lots of different books in it, because reading is one of my most favorite things to do.

If you and your family are on a crowded subway platform trying to get on the subway and you got on but your family didn't, what would you do? My mom says that if that ever happened, you get off at the next stop and wait there for your family.

I think that living in Germany and being home schooled has changed my life. We get to go places that many kids don't.

When I travel, my favorite type of bag is the backpack. It is very easy to carry around (instead of lugging a suitcase).

Someday I want to travel with my own kids, but considering I want to have 8, that might be tricky!

I have a tip: always travel light! Try to leave a little room in your bag so that if you get something along the way, you can carry it yourself.

## Will, age 14

It is important when packing to make a list of just what you are bringing. Once you're done, it's a good idea to review this list. I'm generally an over-packer, and it's quite annoying to lug around stuff you never use. Chances are, out of the six action figures you pack, you'll only use two.

Pencil, paper and books are good to bring. Dice are a personal favorite of mine. Best is to have a kit that includes only things you'll know you'll use.

I like to pack two bags: One backpack for clothing and personal items and a small book bag for the journey and hotel. On an airplane or long car trip, you would use whatever you brought in the book bag to entertain yourself. Don't pack toys both in your satchel and your backpack. Chances are, the backpack stuff won't be used.

It's recommended not to pack electronic games for the journey. In my experience, these make everyone short-tempered and easy to annoy.

It's easy to get frustrated during traveling, particularly with another sibling's behavior. Different people have different ways of handling frustration. My advice is to try and solve problems peacefully.

The worst part of traveling with my family is when other siblings are acting disruptively. The best part is seeing all these awesome things and exploring the exotic places.

Traveling is a skill, which can only be gained with experience. The more you travel, the more you learn what to do and what not to do.

Traveling can be a great experience, but don't try to think about the schedule of events. Follow where your parents lead and don't worry about it; go with the flow and be observant--think "Jellyfish with Eyes" or "Rugged Adventurer."

It's important when traveling to keep your cool. Don't blow your top. Chances are, the people on the floor above can hear you!

Also, it can be easy to start thinking that traveling is just to get from point A to point B, but remember that the destination is the adventure, and the journey is the destination.

### Gabriel, age 13

I have traveled many places with my family. I have been to England, Mexico, Guatemala and elsewhere. I have learned many things; for example, how to pack light, how to have a good  attitude at all times, and most of all always try to be happy at all times.

Hard times matter too  because they teach you how to do things and work (as my dad would say) "as a well oiled machine."

I have traveled many ways: backpacking, bicycling, driving, flying and more. I have enjoyed it a lot. When you are traveling everything matters, the hard times, the good times and all the other times. The good times matter because you build relationships with your siblings.

**Ten Things Good To Have When Traveling With Siblings**

- **Ear plugs**. One thing you should consider bringing are ear plugs.
- **An iPod.** If you have a iPod you can drown out the noise at a campground.
- **A book.** When you are not doing anything it would be good to have a book along. When thinking about the amount of weight a ton of books will make, you could look into buying a reading device, such as Kindle, iPod Touch, iPad or similar.
- **A small backpack.** When you are on a backpacking trip who would want to cary a huge backpack every were? If you have a small backpack with you, you can visit some place without a huge backpack an your back.
- **Toiletries**. In third world countries you will want toiletries because the bathrooms aren't the greatest. Make sure you have a role of toilet paper, a toothbrush and toothpaste.
- **Food.** If you don't have food then you will be hungry soon, so pack a small bar of some sort and you will be fine. I would not pack a chocolate bar because they will melt.
- **A map.** You probably already know but when you're lost it is good to have a map. You could get a paper map or you could get a Garmin or a Tom-Tom or a other GPS device.
- **Spare tires.** If you are on a bicycling trip you should look into spare tires. You're riding down the road one day and suddenly POP!!!!! You have a flat tire! What

do you do now? Well if you have a spare tire then you go through the rodeo of putting on a new tire, but if you don't, you get to carry your bike to the next town. Not fun.

- **Clothing.** When you are traveling by any sort you will want light weight clothing. If you carry heavy clothing it just adds more weight and is hard to get dry.

- **Bikes**. When you are biking you want good strong bikes. If you don't have good strong bikes they will break down. Don't cheap out on your bikes.

210

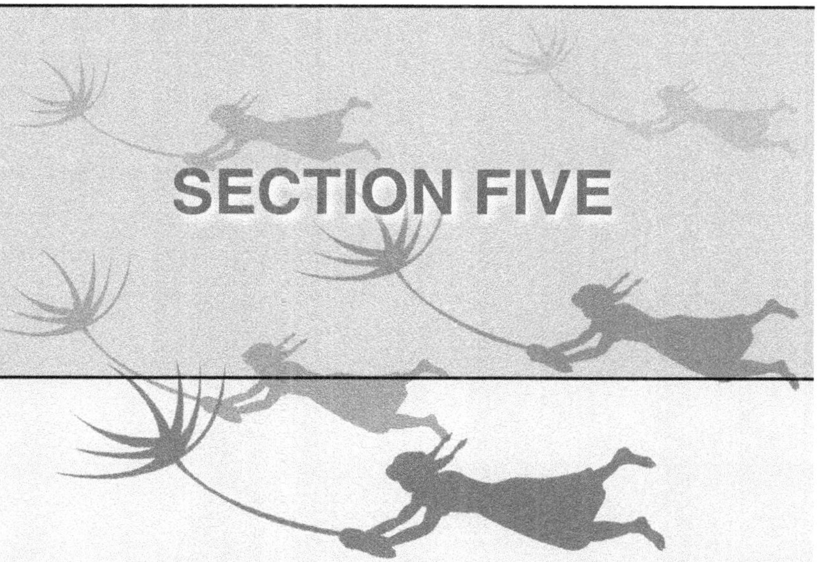

SECTION FIVE

# TRAVEL WITH TEENS

# CHAPTER 22: TRAVEL WITH ALL SORTS OF TEENS

One day, you find yourself looking through the files on the backup hard drive to find baby pictures for the montage you're putting together for your eldest's graduation party.

How did this happen?

It wasn't THAT long ago she was toddling through the lava tube on the big island, when she tripped and skinned her knee. It was the first of many times she fell, and it was the first time you learned to ALWAYS carry band aids and lollipops. You remember it as if it had happened last week.

And now, that tiny, snuggly angel is taller than you, and she is almost ready to walk her own path through this world.

**But will she remember the band aids?**

Relax. If you have been equipping her for travel since infancy, she is going to have the adventure of her life, and the knowledge you have given her will be passed on.

But there is still time to use these last few years to prepare her for her own adventures.

Traveling with teens is undoubtedly easier than earlier years.

Your teen is now completely capable of hauling his own stuff, taking care of his own needs, and quite often, he takes care of the needs of others by cooking, helping with younger kids or doing laundry. Your teen is no longer a ward, as such, but an energetic companion—a young adult who will quickly mature into one of your very best friends.

# The "H" Word

The reason most parents dread the teen years is because of the H-word—Hormones. Hormones have the ability to turn molehills into mountains and back before you can even form a proper response.

The most important piece of equipment in the Gypsy Mama's arsenal to combat teen mood swings is something she has spent years building: **good communication.**

The Gypsy Mama has a track record of being just, fair and calm, which means her teen can approach her with anything that's on his mind.

The Gypsy Teen has such a large degree of autonomy, and thereby ample opportunity for stepping into dangerous situations, it makes communication with parents a vital part of the travel process.

# On the Road Strategies for...

### The Bold Teen:

This child astounds you by her tenacity. She still has friends in every country you've ever visited, and every new person, no matter what their age, race or gender, is her friend. She talks to everyone, and amazingly, everyone talks to her. You have no doubt that she will dash into the world as soon as you raise the gate.

Though the bold teen has had one foot out the door for a few years now, there are some things you can do to further prepare her for her own adventures.

**Let her boldly go where she's not gone before.**

Micromanaging the bold teen will only lead to fights and rebellion. Recognize the changing nature of your relationship, be open to her ideas, and gently give her guidance. If she wants to be out of your direct supervision for a while, make sure she has a trustworthy friend to accompany her and a way to get a hold of you if necessary.

**Let her fail.**

Even if you see the train derailing, let her strive and fail, as long as her personal safety is not in jeopardy.

**Teach her to read—people, that is.**

This is a skill that takes a lifetime to accomplish. But every person, even the whimsical young adult, can get a sense about people. It is important your gregarious teen not fully place trust in every pleasant person she meets at the bus stop—trust is earned and should not be doled out lightly.

**Listen to her instincts.**

Sometimes the bold teen enters a situation she has second-thoughts about. If she trusts that you are on her side, then she knows she has the power and support to back out—and the bold teen will do so.

**Safety first.**

She likes to talk, and talk, and talk. Make sure she knows not to disclose information that could compromise the safety of herself or the family.

**The Introvert:**

You wonder if your introverted child will ever leave the nest because he seems so content to be there. He is the one who hangs on the periphery of a new situation, watching and analyzing, rather than plunging right in.

The good thing about the introvert is he is less likely to go along with the crowd. The bad thing is that he is sometimes overly dependent on the family. The introvert needs to be encouraged (or sometimes forced) to make decisions for himself. But don't expect him to be the leader of the pack, just yet. It takes time. Give him plenty of opportunities to join in any special events when you travel.

## The Emotional:

It is strange to me that people tend to think of girls as "more emotional" than boys, when in reality, boys may be just as prone to mood swings as girls. Having both sons and daughters, I can tell you that gender does not completely dictate how your teen reacts in certain situations.

Both teen boys and girls are undergoing tremendous hormonal changes, and this can affect their moods. Just as you prepared for travel with toddlers, with the mindset of preempting problems, the same can be said for traveling with teens.

The Gypsy Mama will be able to read her child's mood, no matter how old the kid may be, and she can proceed accordingly with tact, caution, or in some cases, firmness. The Gypsy Mama does not ditch her bag of tricks when she has a teen. Matter of fact, the Gypsy Mama adapts to the new stage of life, knowing which 'tricks' work with her child.

## The Perfectionist:

This child may be bold, introverted or emotional, but the perfectionist streak in a teen can be challenging to deal with. While some details, such as researching the destination, are enhanced by her skill, the perfectionist streak can actually inhibit the young adult from  getting the most out of a travel situation.

Perfectionists love order, and travel is messy. With the perfectionist, you will continually be teaching flexibility.

The biggest problem with the perfectionist is that she does not like to fail or to appear less than perfect. When immersed in a new culture, it is extremely helpful to plunge right in—to speak the language, even if you sound like a toddler to the native speaker, in order to truly learn. For the perfectionist, this is a huge roadblock. However, you can encourage your perfectionist by putting him in situations where he must speak the language on his own. It can be something small, such as ordering his own food, or bargaining at the mercado. Or it can be something major, such as allowing him to take a class at a local school. The perfectionist would rather not try at all than try and fail.

The Gypsy Mama will make the most of the teen years by encouraging her perfectionist to try, even if it means failure. She will always let him know that even Gypsy Mamas aren't perfect, and that often times, it is only by picking ourselves up after a failure we can truly fly.

# CHAPTER 23: GETTING YOUR TEEN ON BOARD

Let's face it: Teens are not toddlers, or school aged kids. If they don't want to do something, there's more than a temper tantrum that passes in an hour to deal with. You can't pick them up, strap in them in the car seat and go. In fact, they can walk right out the front door, slam it and walk, or drive, away. What's more, many do.

So what's a Gypsy Mama to do if the family teenager is less than enthused about the rest of the family's dream?

That's a delicate question, one much debated in vagabond family circles: Should parents *make* a teen go?

The Official Gypsy Mama Answer:

Do your *very best* not to make it a power struggle.

## What Teens Want:

In a word, respect. Do you remember what it felt like to be fifteen and fully grown in your own mind but frustrated that no one else could see it? You hated being treated like a "baby." Being talked to like a child drove you *crazy*. You really thought you knew everything you needed to know and you wanted an equal vote in the family and in life.

Of course teens still need parents. The harsh reality is that they *don't* know everything they need to, regardless of

219

whether they think they do. And sometimes as parents we need to put both feet down and be willing to cross our teens for their benefit.

That being said, parents often create battles with their teens that are unnecessary and if we were willing to give a little more, let up on the reins just a bit, and listen more than we talk, perhaps we'd find our teens more willing to do the same.

**Jenn's dad had a great mantra for child rearing:**

"Treat them as much like adults as they can stand."

What does this look like with your teen?

**Easing up on all of the "rules" that you can in favor of coaching his own decision making.**

- Insisting on very little, but making those few things non-negotiable.
- Expecting responsible, mature behavior and acting shocked when you don't get it. "What?! I thought you were a young adult! This is not how young adults act!"
- Giving your child credit, for being the well raised young person she is and treating her accordingly.

## "But You Don't Know My Teen..."

Oh yes we do! Between us, we have three at the writing of this book and as former teachers, we've seen it all; the good, the bad and the ugly.

You may think your teen is a lost cause, but she's probably not.

You may think your teen will NEVER agree to travel with the family, but he might.

We know a 17 year old boy who was arrested for drugs in his home town and was getting into a little trouble. After being *made* to go on a two week family trip to Guatemala, he went home, worked his schedule out with his high school guidance counselor and *moved* to Guatemala to live in a back water town with his uncle and pursue his education long distance while working with his hands, learning Spanish and taking salsa dancing lessons (with our daughter) in the evenings.

We know another 17 year old boy who finished school early, headed south for three months of intensive Spanish lessons with a group of other kids. Then he hiked three days up a river in Honduras to do humanitarian work with an unreached people group.

We know yet another kid, who's sixteen, who studies on line and splits his time between Sweden, Guatemala and Mexico taking chicken buses alone between his parent's homes. I met him in a massage therapy class (for adults) that I took over the winter. He fights with his Mom a lot and he hates babysitting his little sister, but he loves his life. He speaks three languages very fluently.

What do these kids have in common with ours and what must be thousands of others: Freedom, passion and "out of the box" parents.

## Freedom & Passion

Why not offer our kids freedom? Because they'll run amok, right?

Why not let our kids pursue their passions? Because we all KNOW which passion dominates the minds of teenagers, right?

Wrong.

**Freedom is coming, whether you like it or not. Passions are a god given gift.**

Instead of parenting your teen with an iron fist, waiting for the other shoe to drop, expecting the worst and battening down the hatches, why not open your hand?

Why not approach the teen years with a smile and the attitude:

"Look how much you've already done, what are you going to do NEXT? How can I help you? What can we do together? What do YOU want to do with your high school years?"

Five bucks says that the answer to that question will be something other than, "Spend 40 hours a week on school work and play a lot of video games."

Most teens feel trapped (just ask them) and they long in their souls for adventure and excitement; the freedom to live a passion driven life: Hand it to them as your last, best gift.

## What Does This Have To Do With Travel?

Everything. We both know you can't force that teenager to do anything she doesn't want to. You may get her body on the plane, but she'll make the entire family miserable with her teen-a-tude if you don't have her heart and soul on board.

Travel with teens is all about inspiring their passions and feeding them the freedom they crave (in small, carefully measured doses, of course!)

Instead of informing your teen that you're going to be going to Thailand to volunteer in a refugee camp over spring break, stack the deck:

- Begin dialogue about social justice issues
- Watch documentaries about human trafficking
- Find another teen (online?) who's done something cool in the same vein
- Start going out for Thai food
- Find pictures of the beaches of Phuket
- Then ask your teen what he'd like to do about it? Leave the question with him for a few days.
- Then suggest maybe going to Thailand to see for yourself what it's like.
- Ask him what he'd like to see.
- Give him the job of finding the airfare, or the lodging, or choosing the organization to partner with.

If Thailand bombs completely and you get the eye roll and shoulder shrug deal then cheerfully let your kid know that you'll go where ever she likes and do whatever she likes, but she has to plan it. This will create instant interest. We promise.

## Strategies For Energizing Your Teen to Travel:

- Provide three destinations and let her pick.
- Provide a budget and let her plan *anything,* then do it.
- Make a trip out of a passion: European Music Festivals, Extreme Sports, Foreign Languages.
- Create a theme: Give Every Day Tour style.
- Volunteer: doing something your *kid* is passionate about.
- Let them go (gulp) alone. Yes, they can.
- Take a class in something they're passionate about.
- Let them lead. Suggest that *they* take the family on vacation and take care of everything, you fund it, then sit back and watch them learn.
- Get excited, believe in them and cheer louder for their successes and their passions than anyone else does.
- Fight for them. Get in there and argue with the principal of their school for the time off and for full credit academically when they get back.
- Sympathize with their "boredom" with "real life" and be the biggest problem solver on that front that they've ever met.

## Point of View and the Golden Rule

As tough as it is, the teen years require parents begin to see their kids in a new light. You are no longer dealing with children who need to be constantly corrected and given direct orders, but these are young adults, who need clear yet gentle guidance and unwavering support. The Gypsy Mama recognizes this shift in dynamics and begins seeing the adult in the sometimes gangly offspring. The Gypsy Mama hands over the reins whenever and wherever she can.

Yet, this does not mean treating a teen as an equal. The family does have a hierarchy, and friendship between parent and child is something that takes time to mature. The teen still has very real familial obligations--laundry must be done, bags must be packed and planes wait for no one--not even a sleepy teen! However, the most important approach the Gypsy Mama can keep in mind regarding her teen comes from a simple and ancient rule: treat your teen as you would like to be treated.

**Keri Says:**

We joke that our eldest was born 30 years-old, since he's always been uncannily mature for his age. But about the time he could look me in the eyes without standing on a step stool, I noticed that the typical, daily commands began to make him bristle. He always obeyed without a negative word or comment, but something changed in his look and his posture. I knew to continue on that path would be to lose his heart. So, I adopted the golden rule approach. Yes, dishes have to be done, and yes, his siblings need a babysitter from time to time, but the way I ask is no longer a command, but I ask these things as a personal favor. He always says yes with a quiet satisfaction in his eyes, and the bristling has vanished.

## Hannah's Story:

Our family has been traveling for more than three years straight. We've cycled across continents, lived for months on end in tents and campers, rented homes on three continents, and 6 months is the longest we've been in place at any time during our journey.

Our daughter is wildly enthusiastic about almost every aspect of that. She doesn't love sleeping in a tent with her brothers when it lasts for more than a couple of weeks, but she does it cheerfully when the trip requires it. I'm not exaggerating when I say that she never complains. She just doesn't. She's grumpy and has teen-a-tude once in a while, but she's an awesome traveler and she is the picture of flexibility under fire.

However, she doesn't want to go sailing. Her brothers desperately do. Her Dad and I do. She does not. She's not said that she won't and she's willing to try it if we decide to sail as a family. She's trying to learn to like it, but she just doesn't want to live on a boat.

What are we doing about that, when EVERYONE else really, *really* wants to? We're waiting. We're being flexible. We're doing other things.

Since Hannah is so willing to work with our dreams and passions, we're returning the favor. We'll sail after she's off on her own, perhaps. Until then, we're focusing on dreams that *everyone* can get on board with.

Should you force your teen to travel? Perhaps, it would be great for them in the long run, but should you force a particular type of travel. Give your teenager the respect she so desperately wants and take her desires and plans into consideration when you plan your adventures.

# CHAPTER 24: TRAVEL AS EDUCATION

One of the most educational things you can do for your teen is travel. With the world as their classroom, teens will quickly learn languages with an enthusiasm borne of desperation and you'll quit hearing them gripe about the need for math as they're converting currency, figuring out travel schedules, time zones and budgeting.

Sometimes convincing the educational powers that be of the educational value of travel can be a little more challenging.

If your child is enrolled in a traditional school, spend some time with the administrators, pitching the educational value of your travel plans in much the same way you'd make a marketing pitch to a big corporation. If your child realizes that she's going to get full high school credit for skipping school and skydiving over the west coast of Canada, she'll quickly be on board.

What follows are a few ideas for quantifying the "outside the box" experiences that your child will have on the road in a way that will convince the administration that it's been a credit worthy experience:

**Write:**

It sounds boring to most kids, but it needn't be. Writing is the very best way to communicate succinctly what your child has learned and experienced. What kind of writing are we talking about:

- Journalling, first and foremost, this serves as "notes" for later writing projects
- Blogging, have your child create a website and write her life
- Paid Articles, if your child can get published as a result of his travel this will be impressive to school administrators!
- A mini-guidebook

## Photography & Video

Multi-media production has exploded along with the internet. If your child isn't thrilled about writing (or if she is, but you'd like to broaden her skill set) then why not produce a mini-documentary about that refugee camp in Thailand? Some ideas:

- Powerpoint presentations for the classroom
- Podcasts (audio, video or multi-media)
- Create a series of mini-documentaries
- Create a how-to-video about something learned
- Photo essays, for family or for publication
- Submit photos to travel websites, or through a Flikr account

## Social Media

We're pretty careful about our kids' on line presence, especially when they are young children. However, if your teen wants to start a writing or photography career early, the best way for him to network and grow a website is through the judicious use of social media.

Consider these sites to start with:

- Twitter
- Facebook

- Digg
- StumbleUpon
- Youtube
- iTunes (list your podcasts here)

Don't be afraid to set parameters and check up on your teen. The internet can be a dangerous place and there are people who prey on young people who lack judgement

## Social Action

If you're looking for something that will look great on a college applications and give your children a leg up in terms of their experience relative to their less traveled peers, try to inspire your child to social action.

Most high schools now require a certain number of community service or volunteer hours to graduate. For most kids this means working at a homeless shelter on Saturdays, cleaning kennels at the local animal shelter, tutoring kids in the elementary school or volunteering at the hospital on the pediatric ward. These are great experiences, and not to be minimized.

But what if your kid hac:

- Raised money for CoEd Guatemala to provide books for literacy programs and visited the schools in question
- Worked in the clinic in that refugee camp in Thailand
- Visited the child your family had sponsored in India and taken donated supplies to their school
- Cooked at an orphanage in Africa for a few weeks
- Taught English to impoverished kids in rural China
- Which do you think is going to catch the eye of the college admissions officer?

## Equip, Equip, Equip

While travel is inherently educational and kids pick up on a myriad of things adults don't even see, the Gypsy Mama is constantly on the lookout for real-world opportunities for her Gypsy Teen.

Investing a part of the family travel budget in classes or training for your teen will pay off for her down the road. Whether it is language school in Beijing, SCUBA certification in Belize or cooking school in Bologna, any class your teen can take will either enhance her travel experience, count towards high school (or even college) credit, or both!

Make sure you keep everything well-documented (meaning, you even write down the number of hours she spent in training) and keep any certificates (and have them stamped with the school seal, if possible). Travel experiences, volunteer work, classes or training are not only life-changing but are an investment in your young adult's future.

## Resources:

If you're looking for an excellent book on maximizing the educational benefit of travel for your teen, we can recommend no better resource than:

The Global Student by Maya Frost

Some excellent books on creating a passion driven life and education for your teen include:

The Teenage Liberation Handbook by Grace Llewellyn

College Without Highschool by Blake Boles

The Art of Non-Conformity by Chris Guillebeau (not aimed at teens, but required teen reading at our house, nonetheless!)

# CHAPTER 25: A QUESTION OF FREEDOM

## Should You Let Your Child Travel Alone?

In a generation plagued by well meaning helicopter parents, questions like this are loaded with potential for vigorous debate, and that's a good thing. We need to take a long hard look at our kids, and our parenting, especially in the teen years, and ask some fundamental questions before they launch.

- Who is this young person?
- What is his dream?
- Is she ready for the real world? If not, why not?
- What does he most need?
- Is my parenting approach providing those things?
- What can I do differently?
- As a parent, what scares me the most?

The goal of parenthood is to create completely capable, contributing members of society at large and to produce adults who will be part of the solutions, not the problems of the world. To do this, we have to learn to let go.

There seem to be two general approaches to parenting during the teen years:

## Control Focused

The Control Focused parent just *knows* that her teen is going to mess up, big time. She's convinced that rebellion is inevitable, that teen alcohol abuse, sexual promiscuity and probably drug use lurk behind every doorway just waiting to drag her teen into the depths of addictive and abusive behavior.

To "protect" her teen, this Mama sets strict boundaries, keeps a tight grip on the reins, and views her role as that of warden, or police officer. Expectations for conformity and perfect behavior are high. Time to put on a helmet, batten down the hatches and prepare for a rough ride. There will be blood and tears, but these are the teen years and it's to be expected.

The result is often a teen who feels stifled, controlled, not respected and sold short of her true abilities. Since her folks expect the worst, she gives it to them and she rebels against the draconian regulations because she *knows* she's capable of so much more than she's given credit for.

## Freedom Focused

The Freedom Focused parent of teens takes the opposite approach: Sex, drugs & rock and roll are all normal and to be expected. Since we can't control our kids anyway, why try? With these parents, expectations are low and instead of trying to control their teens, these parents seek to become friends with their kids.

The result is often kids who don't live up to their potential because they don't have the gentle pressure of parents who understand that intrinsic motivation waxes and wanes during the teen years. These kids sometimes act out in shocking ways looking for the boundaries that let them know that their parents are there, loving them enough to say, "No" and keeping their unsteady universe in a safe orbit.

There is another way:

## The Confident Coach

Any good coach knows that there are skills that must be mastered in practice sessions. Strength must be built, both physical, mental and emotional before those skills can be perfected; sometimes this means weight training at home. Team spirit and the abil ty to work like a team are built steadily in a hundred small ways before the first big game. After the game, the coach recaps the highlights, encourages the successes, points out weaknesses and sets a plan in place to reduce those weaknesses before the next game.

Parenting teens should be like this.

A good coach is not focused on controlling the every move of every player, on the contrary, he relies on each of them to function independently, to do their individual jobs so well that everyone else on the team can rely on them to be there, catch the ball and run with it, 99% of the time. Failure is an accepted exception to the rule, but the focus of the team is on improving the individuals rate of success in their position.

On the flip side, the game has rules that require conformity. It is the coach's job to teach the rules, show the team members how to use them to their individual and corporate advantage and to cheer them on in the process. It's also the coach's job to enforce conformity to that arbitrary set of rules, for the good of everyone on the team, so that they can all reach their goals and live their dream of playing well and winning big.

Parenting teens should be like coaching.

Teens are amazingly capable. They rise to the occasion when we believe in them and do incredible things with that youthful passion we all wish we could bottle.

The truth of the matter is that you cannot control your teenager. Even if you're controlling the externals successfully, you've got no control over their hearts. The only way to succeed, ultimately, is to win their hearts by becoming their biggest cheerleaders and a very confident coach.

To attempt control is folly. To grant ultimate freedom is to bypass the very real rules of life.

Which brings us back to the question:

## Should you let your child travel alone?

In a word: Yes.

That is to say, you should let your child travel without you. Whether your child is capable of truly traveling "alone" will depend largely on what sort of pre-game preparation you've been up to for the past decade or so.

If you're a recovering helicopter parent, then "alone" might mean:

- A school trip on which you do not go along as a chaperone
- A well supervised "adventure trip" for teens
- A semester abroad program through your highschool
- A trip to Disney with an aunt
- A graduation trip to Spain with Grandma

If you're more of a free-range parent and your child has already stretched his wings, then "alone" might mean:

- Backpacking with other teens in Belize for a week at 14
- Riding a Greyhound to another state to visit friends at 13
- Spending 3 weeks in another country touring with a friend at 16
- Working for 3 weeks on a farm 1200 miles from home at 13
- Flying between continents alone at 16
- Flying without "unaccompanied minor" status between states
- Visiting friends by train between cities at 15

Much depends on your child, her skill and confidence level and your ability as a parent to breathe deeply, focus on the positive and not be ruled by fear

In general, teenagers are a confident and capable lot. As a society, we underestimate them wildly and we Gypsy Mamas strongly advocate a commitment to Jenn's Dad's philosophy: "Treat them as much like adults as they can stand." We think you'll find that they can stand a great deal and they'll embrace the world and live passionate lives of purpose in ways that make you want to stand on your chair and cheer!

## Jenn Says:

At the time of the writing of this book we have two teenagers and have been traveling full time for over three and a half years. Our kids have been a lot of places and have done a lot of "outside the box" things. As a result, we give them quite a lot of freedom.

We've gotten quite a bit of criticism for allowing our teens to do things like travel internationally "alone" with other teens while backpacking, play music gigs in bars in Central America, take on internships half way across the country which require them to live in a dorm-like situation and work 40 hours a week and then travel back and forth across 1200 miles or more alone, riding buses, trains & airplanes between states without us.

Of course we worry about our kids when they're away from us, but it would be unfair to raise them to be world citizens and then keep them from following their dreams as soon as they're ready. The fact is, that our kids can do, and have successfully done, all of those things and are on to planning bigger and better things, like cross continental voyages with their friends, nautical circumnavigations and more.

Be brave as a parent. Trust your kids to rise to the occasion. Turn a deaf ear to the naysayers and expect the very best for yourself and your kids from the world. Then, work hard to give them the skills to succeed!

# Practical Matters: Facing Temptation

If you travel with your children, you're going to come face to face with the good, the bad and the ugly. The hard realities of life are not to be hidden from children. Rather, they're an opportunity to teach, discuss life choices and natural consequences, and allow your kids to live and learn.

When your children branch out and begin traveling alone, there are some very real considerations that you'll need to consider and discuss up front.

## Alcohol

Traveling extensively with children when they are young avoids certain problems that other families might have. In American culture, for example, the college years seem to be synonymous with wild partying. In other areas of the world, however, drinking is a part of the culture, something to be shared with friends and family and enjoyed in a social setting. It is not uncommon here in Europe, where your 16 year-old can consume wine or beer, to see Grandparents raising a glass with their grandchildren. I do realize wild parties occur everywhere in the world, but if you demonstrate responsible behavior, your children are more likely to follow suit.

### What if your teen wants to go to a club with her friends?

Let's be honest. There are some countries I would never let my teen out of my sight. But if you know where she'll be, who she's going with, as well as how and when she'll be getting back, you may consider it. It depends on the community you are in and who she is going with. As long as she knows what precautions to take to keep herself safe, she is (legally) old enough to participate.

## Drugs

When you travel, you and your offspring will come face to face with the reality of drugs. Drugs that are illegal back home are sometimes legal (or in-your-face-available) in foreign countries. Rather than blindly whisk the kids by, talk about it with your teen. The devastating effects of drugs are everywhere you look when you travel—especially in major metropolitan cities. Talk together about what you see, and make sure your child knows that trying a drug once can be the thin end of the wedge, which leads to the destruction of an otherwise bright future.

## Dating

In our family, we feel dating is a waste of time—energy that could be spent learning about new cultures or experiencing the simple pleasures of travel is bogged down by it. We do not believe that casual encounters are at all beneficial for teens. Instead, cultivating strong friendships (even long-distance ones) are much healthier in the long run. While all teens will have romance on the mind at some point (which is fine and normal) dating should be a serious matter, reserved for young adults who have built substantial trust and friendship. Plus, when you are in a foreign country, allowing a teen to date exposes them to significant danger—danger that can be avoided by going out with a group of friends.

## "You Let Your 14 Year Old Do WHAT?!!"

**This winter I took my first solo (parent free) backpacking trip with friends to Belize.**

I've always loved Belize. The food's great, the people are really fun and the scenery is beautiful. But this trip was the best yet.

For one, I had four of the best kids ever traveling with me: Phil,17, David,18, Mel, 16, and Ruthie, 21. Secondly, in the week we had we went to both of my favorite places in Belize: Tobacco Caye and Barton Creek Outpost, in the middle of the jungle.

Tobacco Caye is an idylic island on a beautiful reef that is home to sharks, rays, eels, dolphins, turtles, and hundreds of gorgeously colored fish.

Barton Creek Outpost is surrounded by rainforest with tons of wildlife. It sits on a large freshwater pool, complete with rope swings. Both locations are completely amazing! Even though it rained a few times, my friends and I had a blast!

One of the things I learned on the trip was something my mom has said repeatedly but I never fully appreciated:

**It's usually more fun to go with the flow rather than planning out every step of the way.**

When on a trip, no matter how small, over planning isn't a good way to enjoy your time. If the journey is completely planned it creates stress as you anticipate each new activity and makes it harder to enjoy each day as it comes. During my stay in Belize we planned very little and decided each new step as it came. This allowed us to do some things we wouldn't otherwise have done, like go to Tobacco Caye.

Also: Rental siblings = awesome!

If you don't have older rental siblings I would seriously recommend getting some. They can lead to awesome trips to foreign countries, or the ice cream store on the corner!

$$$ are key!

And finally, I realized exactly what money can buy:

**Freedom, fun, and good memories.**

As soon as I got home I began thinking about how a 14 year old could make a reasonable amount of money on the road. I came up with some ideas and am currently following them and beginning to make money without having to actually get a job. Jobs tend to lock people into a location and take up most of their free time. Not what I want to do.

Instead, I'm developing a freelance writing career online, playing gigs at bars and restaurants as we travel & thinking creatively about how to make and stretch a buck!

When other kids ask me what the most important thing to take on the road is, I usually answer "flexibility and an easygoing mentality."

- It's not always going to go the way you want it to, and sometimes you have to take the hard way to get to where you want to be.
- Always be expecting anything and everything to happen, because it will.
- Be ready for the fact that when you're stuck in the swamp and the flies are biting, it might start to rain.

But also expect that there will be days where you will be basking in the sun, the smell of salt in the air, on a tropical island in Belize on your very first solo trip with some of your best friends and you'll wonder "How can anything go wrong?"

My advice to all travelers is:

**Be ready for the good, the bad, and the ugly. Be ready for everything, and you'll have the adventure of a lifetime!**

# THE WAY WE TRAVEL: HINTS TIPS & GEAR

We are just two among an international parade of globe-trotting Gypsy Mamas; everywhere we go, we meet more and we do our best to talk to them, pick their brains and learn from their experiences.

We'd like to introduce you to a few more Gypsy Mamas who we've asked to share some of their best hints, tricks & gear with you:

## Jennifer D.

**Mother of six:** aged newborn-10 years

**Travel experience:** all over the USA, road schooling wherever they go!

"I wouldn't be able to travel without my sling. I rarely pack a stroller these days. They are too bulky and difficult to use on uneven ground. The sling on the other hand is great for carrying little ones and also works as a nursing cover.

Sunbonnets are a must have. Baby heads burn so easily.

A lesson I learned from yesterday's mistake: Make sure you have a charged battery and large memory card for your camera. You don't want to miss any of those precious moments."

## Abigail Green

**Mother of Ezra**: aged one & a half

**Travel experience:** North America, Europe, Africa... she manages the awesome band <u>Ryanhood</u> and basically LIVES on the road!

1.  **Breastfeed** (I know this isn't what you're looking for, but I mean it)...food is always ready and you don't have to carry it.

2.  **WEAR your baby!** Not only does it feel great and keep a baby happy, it allows you to be hands-free! (Oh, and you can walk through the TSA security wearing your baby which makes taking off your shoes, etc much easier).

3.  **<u>BabyLegs</u>** are a great way to "layer" baby clothes on the bottom. They are basically leg warmers. They look cute under shorts, with just a diaper, or whatever your baby might be wearing....and are super easy to put on and take off.

4.  **If cloth diapering**, I find it easiest to bring just a huge stack of prefold diapers (as opposed to fitted diapers...even though that's what I make :) because they don't take up much room, and they can serve many purposes (diapers, burp cloths, rags, etc). I personally love cloth diapering for a gagillion reasons, including travel reasons: if camping it makes "leave no trace" much easier, you never have to worry about finding a place to buy more diapers, and it's a great conversation piece when everyone stares at you and says, "I didn't even know they still made cloth diapers." :)

5.  If you need to fly with a carseat, **this <u>product</u>** is super convenient. It basically turns your carseat into a stroller/

luggage on wheels while in the airport so you don't have to carry around a huge bulky thing.

**6.** Remember that adults have a hard time with **changing time zones**, so naturally kids will too....it doesn't mean they are having a "bad" or "hard" time adjusting...it just means there is an adjustment happening. Be flexible with bedtimes and wake up times. I'm actually quite enjoying Ezra sleeping in until 10am everyday right now while we are in Michigan. :)

**7. Ignore the question**, "Was your baby good on the flight?" What does that mean anyway? Babies cry when flying and when not flying...they are babies and that's their way of communicating.

**8. Flexibility** with everything, naps included. Naps happen whenever...often in my arms or in a wrap while traveling. I must admit, I really enjoy the snuggle time.

**9. Sink baths** are great. :)

**10.** This <u>portable travel "crib"</u> folds completely flat and can be easily put in a suitcase, under a seat, etc...we are totally diggin' it!

## Michelle O'Brien

**Mother of twins:** 5 month olds

**Travel experience:** from maritime Canada to San Diego, and back, with two babies! I met her on the flight from San Diego to Toronto, she's an awesome Mama!

"Be sure you pack enough milk or formula for the trip, plus a little extra. A little squeeze bottle of dish washing detergent makes cleaning bottles en route much easier!

Definitely pack soothers/pacifiers for your babies, some airlines insist you hold the babies in the upright "burping" position for take off and landing now, which makes feeding nearly impossible. The soothers will help with their ears.

I keep the babies up as long as possible before a flight, this makes it more likely that they will sleep on the plane. I also dress them in jammies to travel so they will be more comfortable and so that I can put them straight to bed when we get home if they're tired.

With twins, I prefer a double stroller to slings or backpack carriers. Be sure your stroller is collapsible and double check airline policies about gate checking before you travel.

If flying with twins be aware that you'll need to sit apart, one adult per child, so that there are enough O2 masks in case of an emergency. Some airlines may not allow you to fly alone with twin babies, so call ahead to check

Make friends with someone on the plane!"

## Dr. Carla Barker

**Mother of four:** ages 9 years to 7 months

**Travel experience:** adventurous train and road trips in America, multiple trans-Atlantic flights, and extensive exploration of Europe.

"The most important thing you can bring is a good attitude-- and it's the hardest to pack."

# Alison Gresik

**Mother of two:** toddlers

**Travel experience:** All over Canada and China, currently on an open-ended world tour!

"Looking after toddlers is hard wherever you are. Given the choice, I'd rather look after them in an interesting place.

Planning is our priority number one when traveling with toddlers: packing snacks and activities, having accommodation booked in advance, researching what equipment we need to bring. Planning helps us meet our kids' needs immediately, whenever they're hungry or bored or tired. Planning also lets us talk to them about what's going to happen so they can be somewhat prepared.

A highlight of our travels was an overnight train ride in China when the kids were three and two years old. We booked a sleeper car and described to the kids what their bunks would be like. We brought dinner and breakfast provisions (instant noodles, rice cookies, water bottles, and our daughter's beloved Pocky). We had comfy clothes and blankets and loveys. We were prepared.

And I still wondered if we were crazy.

But our guide in Nanchang got us safely onto the right car, and the kids were thrilled with their cozy bunks. The rocking of the train eventually put them to sleep, and we woke to the magic of the karst landscape outside of Guilin.

The adventure was that much sweeter because we shared it with our children."

251

## Sharon Hurley Hall

**Who traveled extensively with her toddler and now is Location Independent, with her family, in Barbados**

"By the time she could walk, my daughter had already been to Paris, New York and Barbados - and we had no plans to stop there. Though traveling with toddlers can be a pain (think pushchairs, paraphernalia, tears and tantrums) it can also be a life - enriching experience for both you and your child. Here's why:

The most important thing I gained as a parent was a child's eye view of the world. To a toddler, everything is new, wonderful and worth exploring. Even if you're visiting a destination that you've seen before, by the time you've taken the toddler tour, you will experience it in a whole new way.

Sometimes it is good to sweat the small stuff - or at least to notice the flowers, animals and decorations at the entrance to a famous attraction - and to explore the reasons behind the things we take for granted as adults. If your toddler is talking, expect lots of questions to stretch your brain and challenge your perceptions of history and culture - just try explaining why Robin Hood was good even though he stole what didn't belong to him!

As we travelled, my daughter also gained a sense of the vastness of the world; that there was much more to it than the small corner we happened to be in. She grew to realise that while there are always differences (for example in customs and food), there are also similarities and you can have as much in common with a person who lives half way around the world as with someone who's on your doorstep. I hope that will make her a great global citizen!

## Jessica Montalvo

**Mother of six:** ages newborn through eleven years old, who splits her life between Canada and the United States.

The greatest lesson we've learned, with regard to traveling with toddlers, is to start the process of learning to sit and be content BEFORE the trip at home.

When our children were still in a highchair we would encourage them to be content while they were there.

When they reached about age 2 we would give our child one thing (a coloring book, one color of playdough etc.) and instruct her to sit at the table for ten minutes.

The goal was to teach our toddler to be content while staying in one spot w th limited things to do.

Over time we would slowly increase the amount of time at the table, or sitting in a designated area. We found that this helped us tremendous y with travel, doctor's appointment or anywhere we needed our kids to be content while waiting.

When we fly with our little ones, we carry a variety of activities for them to do, but the great thing is, we don't have to shell out something every 5 minutes because our toddler's attention span lasts longer than that due to the preparing we did at home.

## Rachel Denning

**Mother of five:** aged six months-nine years

**Travel Experience:** They are world citizens who've wandered to Costa Rica, the Dominican Republic, India and back; and are currently driving through every country in North and South America.

"Traveling with toddlers is something that our family has done from the very beginning. Our first real adventure as a family was a 5,000 mile road trip from Utah to Costa Rica. If that wasn't ambitious enough in itself, we did it when our four children were ages 4, 3, 1 1/2 and 3 months old.

Toddler travel carries its own unique challenges- tantrums, potty breaks, all that stuff little ones need- but it also has great rewards. Our philosophy was that if we started traveling while our children were young enough that;

- It would only get easier as they got older and more independent
- they would become so accustomed to doing it that it would be second nature.

Two key ingredients to successful travel with little ones is *flexibility* and *respond-ability*. When those inevitable meltdowns occur, nothing is more helpful than the ability and *willingness* to change plans if needed, and to *respond* effectively to your child's needs in the moment.

Take a short time out to asses the situation- are they tired, hungry, frightened, insecure? Travel can be stressful, but by ensuring that your children's physical and emotional needs are met, you'll find that kids can make great little travelers.

Our children have now grown to five, ages 8, 6, 5, 3 and 1 month, and so far our original hypotheses have proven correct. With each passing month and year, traveling with them seems that much easier, and it has become an event that they not only expect to happen, but thoroughly enjoy doing."

# ADDITIONAL RESOURCES & LINKS

Link to a pattern to sew your own portable tot seat

Link to buy a portable tot seat

Link for our favourite seller of reusable sandwich bags which we use for all sorts of kid travel storage:

Link to the article on kids travel gear that Jenn did for the parent site in July

## LLBean Kids Backpack

 This is our pick for kids day pack and carry-on backpack. The thing to love about LL Bean is their no questions asked, money back, lifetime guarantee. If their backpacks don't live up to your expectations, they'll replace them, period. My kids put this to the test on all continents and we LOVE these packs.

## Travel & Hiking Pack

There are kid sized travel packs on the market, some are better than others. They are sized to fit kids up to about 13 years old. However, if you have a child in the upper age range, consider purchasing a Deuter women's pack that will grow with your child. The best feature of these German designed packs is their adjustable harness system, allowing the packs to be modified for a range of torso sizes... think growing tweens! Our two oldest children sport women's Deuter packs and they are perfect.

## CamelBaks

If you're going to do more than the odd week long trip, and certainly if you're hitting the road in earnest, you want your kids to have camelbak hydration systems. The backpack varieties are our favorites (in fact, our hiking/travel packs have a built in pouch for our camelbak bladders!) Not having to purchase drinks saves a lot of money on your travel budget, each kid having his own portable drinking system ensures that people stay properly hydrated, and the REAL bonus is that your child will be drinking what you want them to drink and it's easier to avoid sugary sodas and unhealthy options. Using a camelbak also means that you're not buying plastic bottles that end up in a landfill somewhere. Save money, stay healthy, keep active, be green... what's not to love?

### The Secret Weapon

In the toddler section we discuss never leaving home without a fully loaded secret weapon. Here are a few of our picks for super special fun things to load it with:

Fish Water Ring Games these tiny versions of the old school water filled ring catch games are perfectly sized for tiny hands and for tucking into your Travel Kit!

Wikki Stix absolutely genius: pieces of string covered in wax in a rainbow of colors. Kids will be entertained for hours bending, twisting and sculpting with these non-toxic, reusable creativity inspiring toys! Buy them in tiny favor sized bags.

I Spy Treasure Hunt Books hours of fun for toddlers through teens, even adults get into these. They improve visual acuity while promoting quiet sitting, perfect!

Etch-A-Sketch pocket sized, of course!

Kaleidoscope the classic tin kind. Who can resist staring through it for hours? Hopefully not your toddler!

**Notice that there are no items that beep, require batteries or are other than kid imagination powered entertainment. With all of the recommendations to limit screen time and media influence on children, it seems wise to encourage free play and creative thought even (maybe especially) when traveling.**

## Jenn's Sources For REAL Kid Sized Gear:

**Keens**: The only shoes our kids wear. Seriously. We get at least a year out of a pair and our kids wear shoes HARD. They are worth EVERY penny.

**REI**: Our boys wear their zip off micro-fibre pants. No matter what your adventure with kids, REI will have the gear you need, and probably at the best price on the web.

**Land's End & LLBean**: What makes these two companies GREAT is their 100% money back guarantee. If a product doesn't meet your expectations they'll exchange it or refund your money, no questions asked, no limits, period. With three boys, that's MY kind of guarantee!

**Little Adventure Shop**:This is a great UK company for top-notch kid's adventure gear. They too have a zero hassle's return policy and they carry the very best of what's out there for kids who adventure for a living!

www.ingramcontent.com/pod-product-compliance
Lightning Source LLC
Chambersburg PA
CBHW021221090426
42740CB00006B/313